The British Bus Heritage

PRESTON'S
TRAMS AND BUSES

GH00577997

By MIKE RHODES

Venture *publications*

FOREWORD

The Author's chronicle of the changing scene of public transport in Preston over the past 90 years will bring to many readers memories of the early days of transport, when the bus was the main source of travel, carrying large numbers of passengers and providing high revenue returns to the Council.

The book aptly portrays the changing pattern of bus services and vehicles as the Authority continued to provide high standards of service through the difficult times of economic change.

Buses thrived in the early days, survived with assistance through the leaner years and now with the realisation that constantly increasing car ownership is creating unacceptable levels of congestion and pollution, public transport may once again return as the future principle mode of travel in urban areas.

I shall have retired in 1995 and this book will serve as a reminder of my 45 years experience of the good and difficult times of the bus industry and I look forward to the future development of Preston Bus in a most opportunistic but challenging environment.

Tom Haldon
Managing Director Preston Bus

February 1995

© Venture Publications Ltd September 1995.

ISBN 1 898432 63 5

Front Cover Illustration

Northern Counties-bodied Olympian number 103 was outshopped by Preston Buses' works just in time to be photographed for the cover of this book. It is seen on Lightfoot Lane working the 32 service back from Tanterton to Town on a bright morning in August 1995.

Photo J. A. Senior

Produced for the Publishers
Venture Publications, Glossop, Derbyshire,
by Mopok Graphics, Glossop SK13 8EH
using computerised origination

CONTENTS

Acknowledgements

In the preparation of this history I would especially like to thank various personnel, past and present, within Preston Bus and in particular Messrs Peter Bell, Nigel Feetham, Derek Fullerton, John Redman and George Orme and I am indebted to former Managing Director Mr Tom Haldon for agreeing to write the foreword. In addition I would also like to thank Jeff Watson and the late Geof Bailey for reading through the manuscript and providing additional material, Janet Renshaw for typing out the original manuscript and last but not least my partner Denise McMahon for her encouragement and understanding. All photographs have been taken by the Author with the exception of those noted otherwise.

Bibliography

In addition to material kindly loaned by the Company the following publications have been used as a source of reference :-
   The Ribble Enthusiasts Vehicle History No. 4, 1977.
   The PSV. Circle Fleet History, 1987.
   The Tramways of Preston by G. W. Heywood – A series of Articles presented in the
       Tramway Review.
   The Leyland Bus by Doug Jack, published by T.P.C., 1977.
   Bus and Coach Recognition 3rd edition by A. Millar, published by Ian Allan 1992.
   The Tramways of Lytham St. Annes by P. H. Abell, J. A. Garnham & I. McLoughlin
       published by Oakwood Press, 1995.
   Various editions of Buses Magazine.

PREFACE

The author's interest in public transport in the Preston area is well known to the staff at Preston Bus. Over many years he has been a frequent visitor to the Depot and Bus station and as a result has built up a detailed knowledge and understanding to provide comprehensive answers to difficult questions sometimes asked about our history.

With all the information being collected together in one publication the author has produced a very useful reference book which should be of interest both to students of transport history in general and to those who particularly follow the development of transport in the Preston area. Local residents will also find the work a reminder of the past and how the town itself has developed over the years.

Looking to the future, the team at Preston Bus will continue to set high standards for the vehicles and services provided for our customers. This publication records in detail the many changes which have taken place over the past 90 years. Undoubtedly further changes will be necessary to keep apace of an ever developing industry and it is our intention at Preston Bus to be at the forefront of any such changes.

The recent buy-out of the Company from the Borough Council and the start made on upgrading the mini bus fleet form the start of a new chapter in the Company's history. I hope readers will find this book of interest and continue to follow the developments at Preston Bus in the future.

P. T. J. Bell
Chairman & Managing Director
Preston Bus Limited

September 1995

Investment in new vehicles continues apace and as this book was being completed a batch of eight Optare Metroriders was being delivered. N421GBV is seen outside the depot before being placed in service.

INTRODUCTION

June 1995 marked the completion of ninety-one years of unbroken ' municipal ' transport operation in Preston. Corporation services were started in 1904 with the gradual introduction of five electric tram routes using 30 cars constructed at the town's Dick, Kerr Works. Motorbus operation commenced in January 1922 and was initially seen as an expansion of the tramway system but by the early '30s the trams were in decline and only buses were operated at the close of 1935. For many years Preston only ever bought Leyland bus chassis, from the nearby Leyland Works and generally fairly local body-builders, with a few notable exceptions, were called upon to complete the vehicles. As recently as 1992, just before chassis production ceased, Preston's bus purchases still came from Leyland Vehicles.

Over the years a total of 54 tramcars and 468 buses (PD3 rebuilds counted as new buses) have been operated, of which only eleven trams and fifteen buses were acquired second-hand. During this time the Undertaking's name has changed six times. At first the trams and initially the buses were owned by the Corporation Tramways Department which later became the Transport Department, denoted for short as P.C.T.D. In April 1974 the name was changed to Borough of Preston Transport Department which later became Preston Borough Transport and then, following deregulation, Preston Bus. When the Undertaking was privatised in April 1993 the name of Preston Bus was registered as a separate limited company but trading under the umbrella of Preston Transport Holdings Ltd.

The fleet livery began as maroon and cream, applied over the years in many different arrangements, but from late 1966 this was radically changed to mid-blue and ivory. Again the arrangement of these colours has changed over the years but the basic hues remained the same in 1995. Although Preston's fleet could probably be considered to be of a moderate size there has rarely been any shortage of interesting vehicles operated. Only in the early 1980s, when the fleet total dropped to a post-war low of 83, did the composition of the fleet take on a somewhat standard appearance, being made up almost entirely of Atlanteans. However, the minibus trend and the resumption of new standard size bus purchases ensured that an interesting fleet was again operated; one which had infact expanded by over 50% in only five years.

For many years the Undertaking had concentrated on serving the townspeople of Preston with nearly all the routes operated being wholly contained within the Borough or the immediate adjoining districts, most of which, with the prominent exception of Penwortham, were eventually absorbed into the Borough by various boundary changes. However, following bus de-regulation in 1986, a veritable explosion of new services was introduced, most of which have since become established routes. Geographically Preston has always been somewhat limited with regards to route expansion, since the location of the River Ribble has mainly confined such activity to the north and west of the town. Nevertheless the development in these areas has been fully exploited and today most areas of Preston enjoy a very good level of service.

Mike Rhodes

July 1995

1. THE EARLY TRAMWAY ERA

(1904 - 1921)

The first passenger carrying horse tramway was opened on 20th March 1879 by the Preston Tramways Company under the sanction of the Corporation. This initial tramway was approximately 2½ miles in length and operated from the Town Hall via Lancaster Road, North Road and Garstang Road then Victoria Road and Watling Street Road to the Barracks. Further horse tramways commenced operation during Guild Week in 1882, which were leased by the Preston Tramways Company to Hardings. These operated thus :- from the bottom of Fishergate Hill via Fishergate, Church Street and New Hall Lane to the Pleasure Gardens, close to the present day Farringdon Park terminus; and from the Town Hall via Friargate, Flyde Road and Tulketh Road to the Ashton district.

Hardings' lease expired on 31st December 1903 and horse trams ceased to operate from that date although, until the start of electric tram services, horse buses were used to maintain the continuity of public services. Preparation for the coming of the electric trams to Preston was a very long-drawn out affair. The first Act of Parliament providing for their operation was passed in 1900. Amongst the lengths of tramway authorised in the Act was a section leading off Water Lane to the site of a proposed car shed near to the dock road; it would also have been very close to Dick, Kerr's Works and the United Electric Car Company (UEC Co) which were situated in Strand Road, where virtually all of Preston's trams were eventually constructed. The 1900 Act also stated that 'the track shall be laid to a gauge of 4ft. 0ins'. However none of the provisions of the 1900 Act were carried out and a new Act was obtained on 23rd June 1902 which stated that the tramways were to be constructed to the standard gauge of 4ft. 8½ins. The 1902 Act listed authorisation for 24 separate sections of tramway totalling some 14 miles 5 furlongs and 25 chains, of which about 60% was intended to be double track. Despite having obtained the necessary powers it was not until February 1903 that the Council's resident Engineer was formally instructed to carry out the reconstruction works. Once work on the infrastructure had begun progress was quite rapid and a car shed and generating station were built in Holmrook Road, off Deepdale Road; a totally different site from that proposed in the 1900 Act. The shed was designed to accommodate 30 cars and had six roads with entry from a special branch in Holmrook Road. There were also associated overhaul works and a paintshop.

At the Town Council meeting of 29th October 1903 it was resolved to accept the tender of Messrs Dick, Kerr & Co for the construction of 30 cars at a price of £472 per car. This was considerably lower than any other tender, with the proximity of the manufacturer no doubt

Dick, Kerr 4-wheel car No. 21 is seen in Fishergate c1906 on the Penwortham to Farringdon Park route. This was one of 26 similar cars which were bought to inaugurate the electric tramcar services in 1904.

(Author's Collection)

This manufacturers photograph depicts Dick, Kerr car No. 30, one of the four bogie cars which were obtained in 1904 for the inauguration of the electric tram services. Note the four bay window construction as opposed to the three bay arrangement on Nos. 1-26.

(Ian McLoughlin Collection)

reflected in the price. These first cars were all open-top un-canopied double-deckers. The original tender had specified four wheel cars but this was changed in January 1904 to 26 four-wheel and four-bogie cars. Numbers 1 to 26 were mounted on Brill 21E 6ft trucks fitted with DK25A motors whilst Nos. 27 to 30 were mounted on 'maximum traction' Brill 22E trucks and were fitted with DK35A motors. The bogie cars had a total seating capacity of 68 contained in a four bay window saloon whilst the smaller cars could only accommodate 48 seats in a three bay configuration.

The first two routes commenced operation on 7th June 1904. These were the services to Farringdon Park, which followed the same route as the previous horse trams, and the service to the Barracks via North Road, which differed from the horse tram route in so much that it avoided Victoria Road and used the more direct route straight along the parallel Watling Street Road. Several

Photographed sometime before the first Great War are 1904 built Dick, Kerr cars Nos. 4 and 24, both in original condition, and seen alongside Miller Arcade in Church Street, heading in opposite directions on the Farringdon Park to Penwortham Bridge (Broadgate) route.

(J. Watson Collection)

more electric tram routes commenced running in the following months; these being the routes to Broadgate and Deepdale on 30th June 1904; to Ashton on 9th July 1904; and to Ribbleton on 26th January 1905. The Ashton tram service followed the previous horse tram route as far as Tulketh Road from where it then continued to the junction of Long Lane (later known as part of Blackpool Road), turned east and continued the short distance along Long Lane to terminate at the junction of Waterloo Road. The Ribbleton route was very direct going by way of Ribbleton Lane and Ribbleton Avenue, with trams turning back near the Bowling Green Hotel, close to the old Borough boundary. The Deepdale route used Deepdale Road and although initially trams terminated in the proximity of Moor Park Avenue the route was very soon extended to the Barracks where it met the Fulwood via North Road route. In effect the two routes formed circular services which became known as the Inner Circle (out via Deepdale Road) and the Outer Circle (out via North Road). Finally, the route to Broadgate again basically followed a previous horse tram route but continued on down Broadgate along the east bank of the river before terminating close to Penwortham Old Bridge.

For operating purposes trams ran through from Broadgate (Penwortham was actually shown on the destination boxes) to Farringdon Park or the Withy Trees Public House, which was situated opposite the junction of Garstang Road and Watling Street Road. Trams also ran to Ashton from either Ribbleton, Lancaster Road or Central Station (now the present railway station but initially known as such to distinguish

it from the West Lancashire station in Fishergate Hill, which closed to passengers in 1900 but remained in use as a Goods Depot right up until 1964). The linking of routes for operational purposes began very early, as did the practice of setting the destination indicator to the terminus of the linked route. This practice was perpetuated right through the bus era and really only fell out of use when linked bus routes (as such) had virtually been eliminated following the various conversions to 'Pay As You Board' (PAYB) operation.

Much of the track laid in the Town Centre, principally in Fishergate, Friargate and Church Street, was unfortunately only single line with passing loops; a situation brought about because of the existing street dimensions. These thoroughfares were not unnaturally the busiest lengths of tramway and Church Street in particular became a bottle-neck since it was used by the Fulwood, Ribbleton and Farringdon Park services. To assist with the smooth running of the trams along Church Street, automatic signals were installed outside the Empire Theatre (outwards) and at the junction of Grimshaw Street (inwards). All of the routes operated were provided with cross-overs to enable short workings to cover only the busiest sections of route. On the Farringdon Park route these were situated at both Skeffington Road junction and at the Cemetery, whilst

A 1904 Dick, Kerr car No. 6 is pictured in Church Street c1910, by which time it had acquired a top cover. This was the busiest length of tramway on the system with the routes to Fulwood, Ribbleton and Farringdon Park all using this thoroughfare.

(Photomatic Ltd)

short working cars on the Ashton service were generally turned back at Powis Road. On the Ribbleton route extra cars were worked as far as the Old England Public House near to the junction of Acregate Lane, where a short section of double track commenced. Both Fulwood services also had cross-overs for short workings which were situated at either end of Moor Park Avenue. The location in Deepdale Road was also adjacent to Preston North End's football ground to which football extras had been run on match days from a very early date. The Ashton route was mainly single track with passing loops apart from in Fylde Road where double track was laid throughout. However, situated in Fylde Road was a particularly awkward bridge which carried the LNW Railway (now the WCML) between Preston and Carlisle, over the road. This bridge presented problems for the Undertaking for many years to come since it was both narrow and restricted in headroom and could only accommodate single line working.

From the outset the tickets were of the bell punch and rack type and were first issued on a geographical basis before being changed to the more usual numerical stage type; this being done when the Department changed its name from *Tramways* to *Transport Department*. Tickets were of different colours for a particular length of journey rather than for different price values; thus if the fare was increased for a particular journey the ticket remained the same colour but the fare printed thereon was altered. Later, during the time that buses and trams operated together, tickets issued on the former carried the word 'bus', whilst those issued on the latter had 'Car' printed on them. Workmen's fares were introduced in 1906 and allowed half fare travel before 8am and between 5 and 6.30pm. Some other ticket facilities available from an early date included child fares and transfer tickets; the latter enabled passengers to book through between certain destinations which required the use of two trams. The basic frequency of most services was usually 10 minutes but that was varied at certain times and last cars on each route left the Town Centre at 11pm which is still the case with the buses today.

In April 1907 a tender was accepted from the UEC Co. for ten top-covers, the design of which provided for five windows, and the cars converted gained an extra two seats on the top deck. A year later five more trams were fitted with the same type of cover. For the coronation of King George V in 1911 three cars were extensively decorated and illuminated; two of these were apparently top-covered whilst the third was one of the bogie cars. In January 1912 plans were formulated to extend the car shed in anticipation of any significant expansion of the fleet whilst at the same time three more cars were ordered from the UEC Co. Numbered 31 to 33 these were single-deck bogie cars mounted on Brill 39E reversed maximum traction trucks with a total seating capacity of 40 which included smoking compartments at either end. They were powered by two 40hp DK9A3 motors and were initially put into service on the Ashton route. At the same time five more cars were fitted with top-covers bringing the total up to 20. However the top-covered cars were excluded from working the Ashton service because of Fylde Road railway bridge and therefore no more cars were converted for a while. Car No. 23 was experimentally fitted with vestibules later that year but this modification was not extended to any more cars at the time due to heavy financial commitments on a track renewal programme.

A re-organisation of through workings took place in 1913 resulting in a somewhat simplified arrangement. The revised workings were then as follows :- Inner Circle; Outer Circle; Lancaster Road to Ashton; Lancaster Road to Withy Trees; Penwortham to Farringdon Park and Penwortham to Ribbleton. The main purpose of this re-organisation was to concentrate the single-deck cars on the Ashton service. Again cars were operated to a basic 10 minute frequency with the Town to Penwortham section enjoying a 5 minute

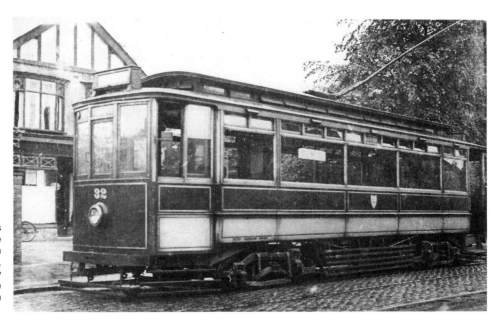

One of a trio of bogie cars purchased in 1912 to work the Ashton service No. 32 is seen at the terminus in Tulketh Road, either in the late 1920s or early 'thirties. The Ashton Route succumbed to motorbuses on 6th August 1934.

In the late 1920s a number of the original cars were substantially rebuilt becoming totally enclosed as illustrated by this view of No. 23 working on the Deepdale circular.

(Ian McLoughlin Collection)

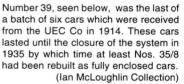

Number 39, seen below, was the last of a batch of six cars which were received from the UEC Co in 1914. These cars lasted until the closure of the system in 1935 by which time at least Nos. 35/8 had been rebuilt as fully enclosed cars.

(Ian McLoughlin Collection)

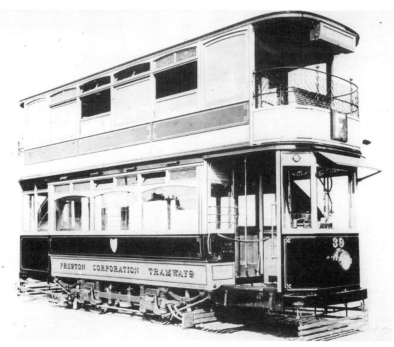

twelve. In December 1913 it was decided to obtain six more new cars and an order was placed with the UEC Co. the following month at a cost of £841 10s for each car. These were open canopied vestibuled cars mounted on UEC 'Preston Flexible Axle' trucks with DK9A3 motors. Numbered 34 to 39 they had longitudinal seats in the upper saloon and seats on the balconies in a 30/22 split.

An Act of Parliament passed on 31st July 1914 gave the Undertaking the necessary authorisation to construct four new lengths of tramway. The most significant of these was for a new route from Corporation Street via Kendal Street, Friargate, Adelphi Street, Plungington Road and Lytham Road to terminate in Garstang Road alongside the Withy Trees public house. Also contained in the Act was the authorisation to construct a tramway along London Road to Walton (or Walton-le-Dale as it is known today)

interval service. As a result of the aforementioned route changes three more cars received top-covers leaving only Nos. 14 to 16 in their original condition. Also at this time discount tickets were introduced which permitted thirteen journeys to be made for the price of which would have terminated just north of the river bridge over the Ribble. However history decreed that neither of these routes would come to fruition since the Great War of 1914-8 put a halt to any expansion of the network. Had they been built it is likely that the two routes would have been linked. Also of some significance is the fact that the 1914 Act conferred powers on the Corporation to run '*motor omnibuses*'. At this time further alterations were made to the car shed and offices to accommodate the extra cars which had recently been acquired.

The war years were not surprisingly a quiet period for developments. In March 1916 Phillipson side-guards were fitted to all cars whilst in June transfer tickets were suspended and later in the year last cars from Lancaster Road were advanced to 10.30pm. In December a collision occurred between two cars in Deepdale Road outside the football ground when a service car ran into a parked special car. Apparently it was normal practice to park the special cars on the inward track between two sets of points, thereby permitting single track running around the obstruction, but in this instance the points had been set in the wrong position and a collision ensued. Problems had been encountered for some time with the reversal of cars in Lancaster Road and consequently in January 1917 it was decided to terminate the Ashton cars in Harris Street. However, in June of the following year a car ran away down the gradient towards Friargate and consequently some consideration was given to further relocating the Ashton terminus to the front of the Harris Library in Birley Street. In the event this proposal was not implemented although some years later the replacement bus service did in fact start from this location.

After the Great War the Trades Council urged the Corporation to make a start on the route extensions which had previously been authorised but nothing was done to this effect. In December 1919 it was agreed to start services half an hour earlier at 6am and to restore running to 11pm. At the same time it was decided to purchase six second-hand single-deck cars from Sheffield Corporation at a cost of £350 each. A further three similar cars followed soon afterwards and the full complement were given the numbers 40 to 48. The nine cars included Sheffield Nos. 125/29, 187/88, 207/09 and 89 and 90 all of which had become surplus to requirements. They were originally open ended, had a seating capacity of 28 and were mounted on Brill 21E trucks. Not long afterwards, in January 1920, a tender was obtained from the UEC Co. to cover in the ends of one car but at a price of £195 it was considered to be too expensive and subsequently it was agreed to have the work done on a '*time and materials*' basis. In September it was decided to carry out similar work on four cars in the Department's own workshops but it is not known whether this was actually done since in 1922 a quotation was accepted from the English Electric Co (as UEC had then become) to equip five 'Sheffield' cars with vestibuled fronts at the considerably reduced price of £64 per car. So the tram fleet had reached its maximum size with all 48 cars in service but circumstances were to dictate a radical change in policy.

In this early 'thirties view one of the ex-Sheffield cars is pictured working on the Ashton service. These are recorded as receiving the numbers 40-8 on acquisition so the application of the No. 26 would indicate that at least some of the cars were later renumbered.

(Ian McLoughlin Collection)

2. BUSES TAKE OVER

(1922 - 1945)

Preston's introduction to municipal motorbus operation started as a modest affair. The residents of the Plungington district had long been complaining that they hadn't a tram service and they continually put pressure on the local Council to provide one. The main drawback, however, was the unsuitability of the main roads in the area, Plungington Road and Brook Street, which due to their restricted width were really unsuitable to carry a tramway. So after much agitation from the residents of the area the members of the Tramway Committee finally decided to embark on the use of motorbuses, which were only seen as an extension to the tramway system and not as a threat. This first bus route was operated as a circular and commenced at the Town Hall running by way of Friargate, Adelphi Street and Plungington Road to Lytham Road then returning to town via the parallel Brook Street; however by 1924 it

was running out and back via Plungington Road. For the inauguration of the service on 23rd January 1922 three Leyland G7s were purchased from nearby Leyland Motors, a transaction which started a long association with this local firm. The G7 was at that time, the most popular of Leyland's 'G' range and those purchased by Preston were numbered 51-53 (CK3446/5/7), which started a new number series following on from the trams. They were fitted with dual-door bodywork built by English Electric and had seats for 30 passengers. Delivered in an attractive livery of maroon and cream, with chrome radiator surrounds, they were fully lined out and carried the legend '*Preston Corporation*' on the sides, although the official company lettering gave the owner as '*Preston Corporation Tramways*'. The vehicles' overall length was just short of 25ft; they had solid rubber tyres, a four-speed gearbox and were powered by a 36hp petrol engine, behind which the driver was seated. A fourth identical vehicle, No. 54 (CK3512), was added to the fleet in June 1923.

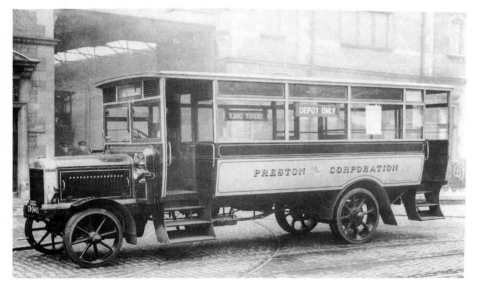

Above: One of the first three motorbuses purchased, Leyland G7 No. 52 (CK3445), stands outside the tram depot in Deepdale Road sometime in the early 1920s. Note the solid rubber tyres and saloon partition inside the English Electric built body, which provided seats for 30 passengers.
(Ribble Enthusiasts Club)

Left: An unidentified Leyland SG7, one of the batch numbered 55-9 (CK3563/4/0-2) which were new in 1924, stands in the garage yard. This view clearly illustrates that two doored buses are nothing new and have been around for very many years.
(Ribble Enthusiasts Club)

Far from there being any thought that the trams were under threat, reconstruction of the permanent way proceeded at a steady pace throughout 1922. The main features were various sets of crossings and points; two sets of which were laid at Mill Bank to enable cars returning from Ribbleton to gain direct access to Deepdale Road and thereby proceed to the Depot. Also at this time the layout under Fylde Road bridge was altered from single to interlaced track. In May 1924 it was decided to equip one single-truck car with a vestibule front and enclosed top deck and appropriately car No. 1 was chosen for this modification. It is known that several of the remaining cars out of the original 1 to 26 batch and at least two of the 1914 balcony cars (No. 35/8) were eventually rebuilt to the same format. Those definitely known to have been modified were Nos. 6, 9 and 24 whilst it is believed that Nos. 3, 5, 17/9 and 23 were also enclosed.

Expansion of the bus services took place on 5th June 1924 when new routes were started, serving the Ashton Lane Ends district and Frenchwood. The former started at the Central Station and took a fairly direct route using Corporation Street and Fylde Road as far as the bottom of Tulketh Brow before diverging left under the infamous 'Danger Bridge' into Waterloo Road. At only 10ft. 9ins. headroom this bridge could only accommodate single-deck buses, but that was not to say that over the following 60 years or so several double-deckers didn't try their hand at squeezing underneath, albeit unsuccessfully; the bridge was redecked by British Rail over the Easter

weekend in 1984 when the headroom was considerably increased. On passing under the Danger Bridge the buses then proceeded to perform a one-way loop via Long Lane to the Lane Ends Hotel from where they returned direct via Tulketh Brow. Of some significance is the fact that this route was responsible for the abandonment of the first length of tramway, since the Ashton tram service was then cut back to Tulketh Road and the section in Long Lane was removed. The service to Frenchwood started out as a circular route running in both directions via Manchester Road and London Road but only serving the upper part of Frenchwood. It wasn't until December 1928 that the route was altered to serve lower Frenchwood on the north bank of the Ribble, at which time it also ceased to run as a circular. It will be noted that the London Road section of this service, like the Plungington Road service, ran over roads which had previously been authorised for tramway expansion. For the inauguration of these services five of the slightly

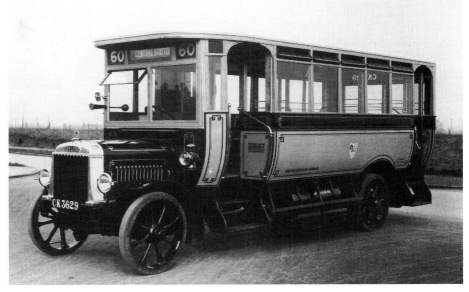

Above: In March 1925 the Corporation purchased two of Leyland's small A13s with 22 seat English Electric bodies. Numbered 60/1 this view shows No. 60 when brand new. A close look would seem to show that the seating is arranged longitudinally inside the saloon.
(Senior Transport Archive)

Right: 1928 Leyland TD1 No. 66 passes between the Cenotaph and the Market Square in the Town Centre heading for Lytham Road, via Plungington Road, sometime in the early 'thirties. No. 66 was one of only two TDs operated by Preston with an open staircase, the other being No. 67 which was bought the following year.
(Senior Transport Archive)

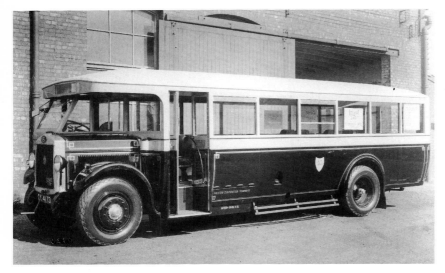

Lion LT1 No. 71 is seen when new in 1929 alongside the Leyland Works. This was one of a batch of four, numbered 71-4, which were used as ambulances during WW2, after which they saw no further use as psvs.

(Ribble Enthusiasts Club)

This splendid view of the interior of the bus garage, taken in the early 'thirties, shows three of the 1932 English Electric bodied TD2s, Nos. 45/8, 50; two of the three Leviathans, Nos. 64/5, and one of the 1929 all Leyland Lion LT1s, No. 71.

(Ribble Enthusiasts Club)

the Arterial Road (today this is the A5085, Blackpool Road). The following year heralded the introduction of the first double-deck buses to the fleet in the form of two Leyland Leviathans, with 52 seat English Electric bodies and numbered 63/4 (CK3746/5). The Leviathan was the first chassis designed specifically for bus operation, rather than bus or lorry, and was 25ft in overall length, the maximum then permitted for a two axle double-decker. It was also the first Leyland chassis type to be given a name. By 1926 pneumatic tyres were fitted to all of Leyland's single-deck chassis but they were not considered to be developed enough for the weight of a fully laden double-decker. However they were available as an option on the Leviathan and those delivered to Preston were all so fitted from new. Whilst Nos. 63/4 were powered by an 8.0 litre petrol engine a further example, No. 65 (CK3907), purchased the following year, had the smaller 6.5 litre engine.

In 1927 Leyland introduced the first of its Titan range, the TD1, which replaced the Leviathan and incorporated many design improvements, such as a cranked and tapered chassis, which served to produce a more passenger friendly vehicle. Preston bought one in 1928, No.66 (CK4050), and one in 1929, No. 67 (CK4172). They were fitted with Leyland's own bodywork built to a lowheight (13ft) specification, with an open rear staircase and 24 seats on each deck. In the tramway committee meeting minutes for June 1929 No. 67 is reported as having cost £1778-12s -6d. This latter vehicle was only one of an order for five buses purchased from Leyland that year, with four Lion LT1 models completing the intake. Numbered 71-4 (CK4173-6)

longer (an extra 2ft 6ins) SG7 chassis were purchased from Leyland, again fitted with dual-door bodywork built by English Electric, but with seating for 36. The significant difference with this model was that the driver was seated alongside the engine which was mainly enclosed in the bodywork; hence the chassis designation SG7, where the 'S' stood for side. The lining out on the coachwork was slightly more elaborate and the Preston Borough coat of arms replaced the 'Preston Corporation' lettering on the sides. They were given fleet numbers 55-59 (CK3563/4/0-2), and Nos. 55/6/9 are recorded as having been modified to seat 32 passengers circa January 1929.

In March 1925 three more single-deck buses were purchased before any double-deckers entered the fleet; these being two of the smaller and lighter Leyland A13s, Nos. 60/1 (CK3629/30), and a solitary SG9, No. 62 (CK3631). All three again had dual-door bodywork built by English Electric, with the former seating 22 and the latter 26. The SG9 had a slightly more powerful engine rated at 40hp. On 10th April a somewhat unusual route was inaugurated which ran from the Cemetery at Farringdon Park to Ashton Lane Ends and vice versa, on Sunday afternoons only, via what was then known as

Rear offside view of 1931 English Electric bodied Leyland TD1 No. 52 taken when brand new and clearly showing the elegant lines of the coachwork to good effect. Note the rear destination aperture which was a specified feature of certain pre-war models.

(P. Hesketh collection)

Centre right: One of the three English Electric balcony cars acquired form Lincoln Corporation in 1929 is seen outside Miller Arcade on the Ribbleton service with one of the rebuilt 1904 cars behind.

(Ian McLoughlin Collection)

they were fitted with Leyland's own front entrance bodywork with a lower floor level which improved entry and exit access, and they had seats for 35 passengers. They were powered by a 5.1 litre petrol engine and transmission was through a four speed sliding mesh gearbox. All four were withdrawn in October 1939 and converted for use as ambulances during the Second World War, being stationed at various strategic sites around the town.

Returning to the tram fleet, Preston undertook to construct three new double-deck cars made up from parts taken from withdrawn cars. By 1927 at least five of the 1904 cars and two of the ex-Sheffield cars were out of service and these were used as a source of parts for the new cars. Numbered 30, 40/2 they were actually constructed to a lowheight specification for use on the Ashton service under Fylde Road railway bridge. The final three cars operated by Preston, which had been built by English Electric (Dick, Kerrs) in 1919, were bought second-hand from Lincoln Corporation in June 1929, thereby returning to their place of origin. These received the numbers 13/8 and 22, filling in some of the gaps created by the withdrawal of some of the older cars. The ex-Lincoln cars had bodywork of a lowheight design with open balconies mounted on 6ft 6ins Brill 21E trucks which were powered by DK30B 40hp motors and consequently they were suitable for use on the Ashton

This Depot interior view, taken circa 1930, depicts 1912 bogie car No. 33, Preston rebuild No. 30 and rebuilt balcony car No. 38. Note the difference in height between the two double-deck cars with No. 30 having been specially built to a lowheight specification for working the Ashton service.

(Ian McLoughlin Collection)

Lined up inside the bus garage are seven of the batch of ten Leyland TD2s which were new in July 1932. From left to right they are Nos. 42, 47, 41, 43-5, 48. These particular buses led an interesting life whilst with Preston with at least two being loaned to the LPTB c1941 and several receiving new E. E. bodies in early 1940.

(Preston Bus)

route. Meanwhile the bus fleet continued to expand apace with the acquisition of two more Leyland TD1s in 1931, which repeated the first fleet numbers, 51/2 (CK4601/2), since the original vehicles with these numbers, CK3446/5, had been withdrawn earlier in the year. In the event they were fitted with English Electric H29/24R bodies although the original tender from Leyland Motors, which was initially accepted, had quoted for the complete vehicles.

At the end of 1931 the bus fleet had totalled just 19 but four years later it had greatly expanded to 71. Although the possibility of trolleybus operation had been pursued, and in fact an Act of Parliament dated 27th March 1931 had given the Corporation the necessary powers for their use, it was the motorbus that was to replace the electric trams. Modernisation of the fleet began in July 1932 with the acquisition of ten Leyland Titan TD2s with H29/24R English Electric bodies, numbered 41-50 (CK4637-44/6/7). These buses led a far more interesting existence than most of the pre-war Titans. After only some 7½ years in service several were fitted with new bodies, again built by English Electric, but with the addition of one extra seat on the lower deck. Those so dealt with were Nos. 41/3-7/9. At least two of the batch were loaned to the London Passenger Transport Board for a few months at the turn of the year, 1940/1; those so recorded being Nos. 42 and 50, both of which had a commemorative plaque installed in the lower saloon, inscribed 'London 1940-41'. No. 49 is also thought to have spent some time with the LPTB, having gone south almost immediately after re-bodying. On their return to Preston Nos. 42 and 50, along with 48, then went on loan to Lancashire United Transport, with the last not returning until the beginning of 1944. The whole batch, except No. 50 (withdrawn in 1947), was withdrawn in 1951 being replaced by some of the first

Leyland PD2s to enter the fleet. Part of the same order were Nos. 75-8 (CK4648-51), four Leyland Lion LT5s with B32R English Electric bodies. These were originally powered by 5.1 litre petrol engines but were later converted to 'oil' (diesel) engines. Whilst No. 75 only lasted until 1941, passing to the Auxiliary Fire Service for use as a mobile canteen during the war years, the other three continued in service for several years after the war. Number 76 was converted to a mobile library bus for the Borough and was used as such from September 1948 right through to November 1966, when it was finally replaced by a purpose built vehicle. During this time, CK4649 (ex-76) was a common sight outside the town's Harris library, where it would be restocked with books before taking up its various sites around the town. It is now undergoing full restoration in Wiltshire.

So far none of the services operated have been referred to by route numbers. Apart from a brief period in the mid 1920s, when route numbers were used on the trams, Preston was one of the few towns to adopt letters (mnemonics) to indicate the individual routes. It has not been recorded exactly when these were first used but by 1926 the tram routes were using the following :- A for Ashton, D for Deepdale (Inner Circle), F for Fulwood (Outer Circle), FP for Farringdon Park, P (changed to BR in 1935) for Penwortham (Broadgate) and R for Ribbleton. The letter O was also used for 'Other'

Four more Leyland Lions of the LT5 marque, but with 32 seat rear entrance English Electric built bodies, were purchased in July 1932 as depicted here by No. 77 seen when new. This particular vehicle went on to complete eighteen years service with Preston.

(R. Marshall)

workings such as Specials etc. Initially the bus routes do not appear to have used numbers or letters and it is not before September 1932 that the timetable booklet refers to the then bus services as PL for Plungington (Lytham Road) and A for Central Station to Ashton Lane Ends, whilst FR for Frenchwood appears for the first time in the following year's timetable, dated September 1933.

The motorbuses purchased from 1932 onwards were used mainly to convert existing tram routes to motorbus operation and not for further expansion of the route network. The first tram routes to succumb to the more flexible bus were the routes to Penwortham (Broadgate) and Farringdon Park, on 4th July

1932 Leyland Lion LT5, CK4649 (formerly No. 76), seen in its guise as a mobile library bus in Jacson Street some time in the 1950s, a duty which it performed for some eighteen years from September 1948 to November 1966. The vehicle has been saved and is now undergoing complete restoration as a long-term project.

(Author's collection)

1932. The Farringdon Park route was probably chosen first because its track was in great need of renewal, although a few trams were apparently operated as extras to the buses for a short while after the official closure date. From 19th September a bus service started running to Ribbleton in conjunction with the tram service. This was initially run on an alternate basis interworked with the tram service but with the buses terminating in Chatburn Road. By November 1933 only a few tram journeys remained and although these continued well into the following year the bus service eventually won the day. However, not long before the trams ceased altogether car No. 6 came off the rails near the County Arms after 'running away' whilst working back from Ribbleton to town. As a brief interruption to the tram conversion programme, a separate bus route from that operating on Sunday afternoons commenced running between the Cemetery and Lane Ends (Ashton), on M-S, using the letter C, as opposed to LEC for the former. This service was routed off the 'Arterial Road' at its junction with St. Gregory's Road and followed a series

of back roads before rejoining the Arterial Road (Addison Road) close to the Lane Ends terminus.

In March 1933 Preston took delivery of five new buses which were given the registration numbers CK4703-7. These comprised three Leyland Titan TD2s, Nos. 68-70; a further Lion LT5, No. 79; and the Undertaking's solitary Tiger, TS4 No. 80, all of which were bodied by English Electric. As built, Nos. 68/9 were of H28/24R configuration, whilst No. 70 had two fewer seats on the top deck. Both of the single-deckers were rear entrance 32 seaters. Part of the same order, but not received until October, was a further TD2, No. 53 (CK4702), whilst Nos. 54-9 (CK4792-7) were a batch of TD3s which followed in November. The TD3 was longer than its predecessor by 1ft and its design had

was not a straightforward affair. At first it looked as though Fylde Road railway bridge would save the day for the trams since the Traffic Commissioners initially refused permission to operate double-deck buses underneath it. However a second application, which also included an alteration to the routing in Ashton, was later accepted and as a result ten lowheight English Electric bodied TD3s were purchased especially to operate the service. Two years earlier, in 1932, Leyland had experimented with the semi-automatic torque converter which was the first automatic transmission for buses in Europe. Buses so fitted usually had the badge 'Gearless Bus ' affixed to the front of the radiator. The batch taken by Preston was fitted with converters and entered service as numbers 1 to 10 (CK4921-30), which started a trend to number lowheight buses accordingly. The English Electric bodies had seating for 26 on each deck and besides having separate destination and route letter boxes at the front they also had side destination screens over the open platforms. Virtually all of Preston's new buses were fitted with side destination equipment right up until 1984. Number 4 was withdrawn after an accident in 1939 and Nos. 1 and 9 were rebodied by Croft in 1945. Numbers 2, 5 and 10 were licensed for twelve standing passengers in January 1942 to help ease the overcrowding which was a common occurrence during the war years. As a result of the conversion of the Ashton service to motorbus operation more trams were

advanced somewhat in that the new, deeper radiator had smooth parallel sides as opposed to the less stylish tapered variety of the TD2. Numbers. 50/3-9 and 70 all had oil engines from new and were amongst the first such powered double-deckers in the fleet. Most, if not all of the batch numbered 41-9 along with No. 51, were later similarly converted. Nos. 53 and 69 were rebodied by English Electric just before the start of hostilities and whilst Nos. 54-9 all originally had English Electric bodies with H29/24R seating three of these, Nos. 55/6/8, were also later rebodied, in March 1945, by the Glasgow firm of Croft, at which time they were upseated by two on the top deck. Meanwhile in June 1933 the Corporation had started using TIM ticket machines and by March 1939 these appear to have ousted the former bell punch machines.

The tram to bus conversion programme resumed on the 6th August 1934 when the Ashton route was the recipient of a batch of new buses although the conversion

Croft rebodied Leyland TD3 No. 56 is seen on the Ashton Lane Ends stand in Harris Street in the 1950s. No. 56 was amongst the last pre-war Titans in service, not being withdrawn until 1957.
(R. Marshall)

Ten lowheight TD3cs were purchased in 1934 to replace the trams on the Ashton service. This view shows No. 6 newly built at the English Electric factory.
(Ribble Enthusiasts Club)

Preston's solitary Leyland Tiger TS4, CK4707 (formerly No. 80), is seen masquerading as a promotional advert for National Child Safety week in March 1954.
(Ribble Enthusiasts Club)

Croft rebodied 1934 Leyland TD3c No. 1 seen in the garage yard in 1954. The chassis was 23 years old when No. 1 was withdrawn in 1957 whilst the Croft body had replaced its original English Electric body in 1945.

(R. Marshall)

The last of the 1934 lowheight English Electric-bodied TD3cs to remain in service, other than rebodied No. 1, was No. 3 which in this view is parked on the Ashton A stand in Birley Street.

(R. Marshall)

linked together forming a complicated pair of circular routes.

Although buses took over the running of football specials after the withdrawal of the trams the first dedicated bus service was started from Kendal Street in August 1934. By March 1938 special buses also operated from the Cemetery, Carlton Drive (Frenchwood), Aqueduct Bridge (Lime Kiln P.H.) and Pedders Lane, Ashton. Curiously, none of these seem to have been running at the start of the 1937/38 season since they are not shown in the November 1937 timetable. Perhaps it was North End's success that season, they finished third in Division One and won the FA Cup, that prompted the introduction of further services during the course of the season. In March 1935 the Department made two rather unusual purchases in the form of two second-hand Titans which were numbered 60/1 in the Preston fleet. Number 60 (OF3959) was a Leyland TD1 with Leyland's own lowheight bodywork which had originally operated with Birmingham Corporation (as their No. 99) from new in January 1929 and was in fact later purchased by that concern, in 1932. It was subsequently fitted with an oil engine and passed back to Leyland Motors in February 1935 before being acquired by Preston the following

withdrawn which included the Preston rebuilds. Number 30 was acquired by Lytham St. Annes becoming No. 56 in the Fylde coast fleet where it survived until closure of the system in 1937.

At this time the letter 'A' was used for two completely separate routes simultaneously; the only common factor being that they both served Ashton, albeit different parts of the district. As briefly referred to when the Ashton tram route was converted to motorbus operation the opportunity was also taken to alter the route with the buses returning to town via Pedders Lane and Egerton Road back to Tulketh Road. However the route letter situation remained unaltered except that by the following year the Pedders Lane route was known as the 'Ashton Main Route'. The day after the Ashton tram route was converted to motorbus operation a second route started running from the Central Station to Ashton Lane Ends which was lettered B. Routes A and B to Lane Ends were month. After a relatively short time in Preston colours it was sold to the Scottish operator Central SMT in 1937. Number 61 (TJ3278), meanwhile, was originally built as a TD3 , again with Leyland's own bodywork, and was initially used by Leyland as a demonstrator from new in October 1933. It was later converted to a TD3 with a torque converter and an oil engine, and was acquired by Preston at the same time as No. 60, but it lasted a considerable time longer not being withdrawn until 1950. It was also the first bus owned to be fitted with a Clayton Dewandre saloon heater and it spent a lot of its working life on the cross-town service (C).

The end for the trams finally came on 15th December 1935 when the first two electric tram routes, the D and F circulars, were converted to motorbus operation. The trams finished with little ceremony and there is even some speculation as to which was the last car in service although it is claimed that this honour befell car No. 4. These two routes had still required the use of some 20 cars and a similar number of new buses was required to complete the conversion programme. Consequently in November and December 1935 a large intake of Titans comprising 22 TD4cs was pressed into service. These were Nos. 11-14 (RN7701-4) which carried all-metal H30/24R bodies constructed by Leyland and Nos. 15-32 (RN7705-22) which were fitted with H28/26R composite bodies built by English Electric. The traditional method of body building in the 'twenties and early 'thirties had incorporated wooden pillars and framing covered by metal panelling. In October 1932 a TD2 demonstrator was built with a six bay all-metal

highbridge body and this design became available to operators in 1934. The advantage of the all-metal body was its longevity, virtually eliminating the need to rebody vehicles since the latter had a life span more in keeping with that of the chassis. The Department's policy at that time was to divide bodywork orders between Leyland Motors and the town's own English Electric Co. Numbers 11-32 comprised the biggest single order for buses ever placed by Preston Corporation under that or any subsequent name. When new the Titans wore the fully lined out maroon and three cream bands livery but with all except one seeing service into the 1950s the post-war livery of plain maroon and cream, without lining, eventually replaced the former. Also part of the same order were two Leyland Lion

1935 English Electric bodied Leyland TD4c No. 21 is seen parked in Deepdale Road on Football Special duty with one of the 11-4 batch behind. This view dates from the early 'fifties when North End was in the First Division and attracting very big crowds.

(R. Marshall)

Seen when newly built for Birmingham City Transport in January 1929 is Leyland TD1 OF3959 which joined the Preston fleet in March 1935, becoming No. 60. However it was withdrawn as early as 1937 passing on to Central S.M.T.

(Senior Transport Archive)

Above: This view shows the four Leyland TD4cs, Nos. 11-4, with an all-metal body construction which were purchased in November 1935 as part of a much larger intake of new vehicles to replace the last of the trams.

(P. Hesketh collection)

Number 14, one of the four TD4cs pictured above, is seen in virtually original condition on the Holme Slack stand in Jacson Street, sometime in the early 1950s.

(R. Marshall)

In this early 'fifties view, 1935 English Electric Leyland TD4c No. 28 has lost its beading below the upper-deck windows and consequently only sports two cream bands. It is seen on the Moor Nook stand in Birley Street.

(R. Marshall)

1935 Leyland Lion LT7c No. 82 is seen on the Gamull Lane stand in Harris Street in the early 1950s. No. 82 has lost its 'gearless bus' badge which may indicate that the torque converter has by now been removed. Both Nos. 81/2 survived in service until 1954 when the need for single-deckers came to an end with the re-routing of the Ashton B away from the 'Danger Bridge'.
(S. N. J. White)

English Electric-bodied 1938 Leyland TD5c No. 37 and 1935 TD4c No. 24 are seen in Deepdale Road awaiting the crowds at the end of a Division One match, sometime in the early 'fifties.
(R. Marshall)

New in 1932 Leyland TD2 No. 45 is pictured after receiving its second English Electric body in 1939/40. Only Nos. 42/8, 50 of the batch are thought not to have been rebodied.
(R. Marshall)

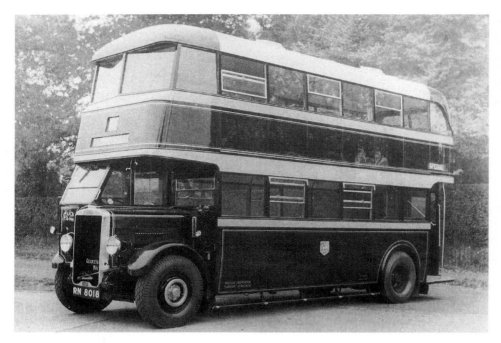

1936 English Electric bodied Leyland TD4c No. 62 pictured when brand new. Note the then common half depth opening windows and the arrangement of the separate route letter and destination apertures, which were a feature of many of the pre-war models.

(R. Marshall)

LT7cs, Numbers 81/2 (RN7723/4), with that manufacturer's own B38R bodywork. These were somewhat unusual in that torque converters were rarely fitted to the Lion range. These two buses, along with Nos. 76/9, 80/3, in common with many other single-deck buses during the war, were fitted with perimeter seating for 28 passengers with standing room for a further 28, for a period between 1941 and 1946, to provide additional capacity on routes serving factories involved in the war effort where normally only double-deckers were employed.

The vast changes in rolling stock which took place in the period 1932-5 had necessitated various alterations to the garage. Back in March 1930 the Borough Surveyor had requested that plans be prepared for an extension to the motor bus garage which was to be linked to the tram shed. The following January the tender received from the local firm of H.H. Topping was accepted to carry out the approved work. Two years later it was resolved to concrete-in half of the tram shed and open up the dividing wall into the bus garage. The developments of the early '30s were finally completed in 1935 when the remainder of the tram shed was concreted-in. These alterations reflected the policy of tramway replacement during which time 54 Titans, 7 Lions and a solitary

In 1937 Preston ordered six new buses comprising five TD5cs and a solitary Lion. No. 83 was an LT7 fitted with a torque convertor and a 38 seat English Electric body.

(Ribble Enthusiasts Club)

Tiger were purchased from Leyland Motors, which besides seeing out the trams had also eclipsed most of the first generation of buses.

Before the Second World War four more completely new services were started. The first of these was introduced on 17th February 1936 and ran from the Town Centre to Holme Slack via a series of back roads. Lettered HS, this particular route was altered very little over the years and in 1995 it still followed more or less exactly the same route from St. Paul's Road to the terminus opposite Lily Grove. On 1st April 1937 an agreement with Ribble Motor Services came into operation whereby the latter could pick up passengers going into town on London Road to compensate for the absence of any Corporation services which had been lost some years earlier with the re-routing of the Frenchwood service. At the same time it is thought that there were similar arrangements made concerning Fulwood and Ribbleton. The first service to terminate at Gamull Lane started running on the 15th April, lettered GL; it followed a similar route out of town as the service to Holme Slack but instead of using St. George's Road it traversed the parallel St. Thomas's Road before making a left turn into Deepdale Road and then proceeding via Watling Street Road to the junction of Gamull Lane. Right from the introduction of this service certain journeys were extended the half mile or so to the Fulwood Row / Longsands Lane junction, where the service terminated in delightful countryside. In November a third route to Lane Ends Ashton, lettered C, commenced running from the Town Centre. This service was routed along Brook Street which had been used some years earlier by buses on the very first motorbus route to Lytham Road. The latter had ceased to be used as a terminus by the PL in July 1933, when the full service was extended to Boys Lane. Following many requests from residents, circa March 1939, the PL was further extended along Black Bull Lane to turn back at

the junction of Queens Drive, although alternate buses continued to turn round at Boys Lane for many more years. The final pre-war service to commence running was that to Moorside (later known as Moor Nook) on 10th July 1939, which was lettered M.

The services operating immediately before the 1939-45 war were as follows :-

A	(Main Route) Town Centre and Pedders Lane Ashton (former tram route)
A	Central Station and Ashton Lane Ends via Maudland Road / Waterloo Road
B	Central Station and Ashton Lane Ends via Bow Lane / Tulketh Brow
BR	Town Centre and Broadgate (former tram route)
C	Cemetery and Lane Ends (Ashton)
C	Town Centre and Lane Ends Ashton
D	Deepdale (Inner Circle) via Town Centre (former tram route)
F	Fulwood (Outer Circle) via Town Centre (former tram route)
FP	Town Centre and Farringdon Park (former tram route)
FR	Town Centre and Frenchwood
GL	Town Centre and Gamull Lane or Longsands Lane
HS	Town Centre and Holme Slack
LEC	Cemetery and Lane Ends via Arterial Road (Sunday pm only)
M	Town Centre and Moorside
PL	Town Centre and Boys Lane or Queens Drive (via Plungington Road)
R	Town Centre and Ribbleton Chatburn Road (former tram route)

To complete the story of vehicle development before

1937/8 English Electric Leyland TD5cs Nos. 33/6 are seen in the garage yard in their modified form for use as grandstands during the 1952 Guild. They were both disposed of in this state after the Guild had been concluded.
(P. Hesketh collection)

Pictured in January 1940 when brand new are Leyland TD5cs Nos. 4 and 38, the former with a 53-seat lowheight body and the latter with a 55 seat highbridge body. Note the lack of headlights and the white painted mudguards which reflect the wartime restrictions which had been introduced around the time of their entry into service.

(Preston Bus)

the war another fourteen vehicles were added to the fleet strength between 1936 and 1940. Numbers 62-4 (RN8018-20) were three more Leyland TD4c models with English Electric H30/24R bodies, purchased in September 1936. These buses were amongst a number of gearless Titans, recorded to be Nos. 1, 3, 4, 8, 11-4/6/9, 23/5/6/8/9, 32-40, 62-4, which were fitted with crash gearboxes in the early post-war period. Numbers 62/4 were later upseated with the addition of two more seats on the lower deck. Interestingly No. 62, following withdrawal in November 1955, passed to the Fylde concern of F.G.Timms who converted it for use as a cattle transporter in which guise it returned to the Deepdale garage on several occasions for electrical attention. December 1937 saw the purchase of a further Leyland Lion, No. 83 (RN8353), again of the LT7c marque and with English Electric B38R bodywork, whilst Leyland TD5cs Nos. 33-7 (RN8348-52) formed part of the same order and followed shortly afterwards, in January 1938. Again English Electric bodywork was carried with seating for 30 passengers upstairs and 24 downstairs. Interestingly, for the 1952 Guild, Nos. 33/6 were rebuilt for use as mobile grandstands for viewing the various processions. For this purpose they had all the glazing removed from the nearside and the open window apertures were enlarged. Neither bus saw any further use with the Corporation and both were disposed of to a local dealer in January 1953 still in their modified state. Four more TD5c vehicles were ordered in May 1939 but these did not enter service until December, three months after the start of hostilities. Numbers 38-40 (RN8885/6/4) had Leyland H29/26R bodies whilst

the fourth was numbered 4 (RN8887) and was a replacement for 1934 TD3c Titan No. 4 (CK4924), which had been damaged beyond repair in an accident in April. Like the vehicle it replaced, RN8887 carried a lowheight body of L27/26R configuration. The final pre-war bus was No. 65 (ACK224) which entered service with Preston in January 1940. The chassis was built in January 1939 as a TD6 prototype (which was indigenous only to Birmingham City Transport) but was later rebuilt as a TD7, before receiving its Leyland H30/26R body. Number 65 was the last new bus to be adorned in the three cream bands livery with *full* lining out.

At the committee meeting held on 16th October 1939 it was resolved to install a 'Producer Gas Plant' in one bus but it has not been recorded whether this was followed through or indeed which vehicle might have been used. Somewhat interestingly during the war years the fleet was dispersed to prevent serious damage during air raids. Whilst a third of the fleet remained at the garage the rest was outstationed in two equal sized groups; one on waste ground off St. Stephen's Road, near Preston North End's football ground and one near the Gas Works off Moor Lane. Another innovation was the installation in 1944 of a steam pipe system in the garage yard which could be connected up to the radiators of parked vehicles to prevent freezing up in the winter months, since many of the buses still had to be parked out in the open. During the war only three buses were withdrawn, these being TD1s Nos. 52 and 67, both in 1940 and Lion 75, in March 1941. Both the TD1s were sold to Cumberland Motor Services becoming their

Number 65 was the 1940 built Leyland TD7, withdrawn in 1958, which is seen here parked in the garage yard in the mid-'fifties. This was the last bus received in the maroon and cream livery with full lining out.
(R. Marshall)

In 1945 Croft rebodied three of the 1933 batch of Leyland TD3s, Nos. 54-9, which originally had English Electric bodywork. One of the trio, No. 55, is pictured on the Moor (garage yard) in 1954; the others so treated were Nos. 56/8.
(Author's collection)

Nos. 20 and 8 respectively. They were then rebodied by Northern Coachbuilders with utility lowheight bodies in 1943/4 with No. 8 receiving a Gardner 5LW engine at the same time. Meanwhile No. 75 was loaned to the Streets and Buildings Committee for use as a mobile canteen. A few months later it was requisitioned by the Home Office and supported the war effort for the full duration. In July 1945 it was returned to the Transport Department but did not see any further use as a psv. The fleet size remained static at 74 from 1941 to 1946 and other than wartime modifications to buses such as headlight covers and wire mesh grilles over the windows etc. Preston, like most other fleets, had to make do and mend during the hostilities.

As previously recorded the final event covered by the period under review was the re-bodying of several of the 1933 TDs by Croft in early 1945. It has been suggested that wartime Croft bodies, unusually of six-bay construction, were in fact major rebuilds of existing bodies. The next period in the Department's history was to be one of fleet modernisation and expansion which coincided with the new generation of post-war Titans introduced by Leyland Motors from 1946 onwards.

3. THE POST WAR TITAN ERA

(1946 - 1968)

As long ago as early 1941 an order had been placed with Leyland Motors for the supply of twelve complete double-deck buses. This order was later revised and in the September of 1946 modernisation of the fleet at last began with the delivery of the first of ten Leyland PD1s. The PD1 was powered by a 7.4 litre direct injection engine and had a wider radiator than the TD models. Numbers 52, 84-89 (ARN394/88-93) were actually built at Walter Alexander's works in Falkirk to Leyland's design and were H30/26R in configuration, whilst the balance of the order, comprising lowheight examples Nos. 60/6/7 (BCK25-7), followed in December and were constructed at Leyland's Farington Works to the L27/26R configuration. In common with pre-war deliveries front and side destination screens were a distinct feature but these were to a larger format and some buses, which had been fitted with the narrower blinds, originally had the top and bottom of the blind aperture masked off. Later the policy of numbering lowheight buses from 1 to 12 was re-adopted and consequently Nos. 60 and 66 were renumbered in August 1958 to 8 and 12 respectively. Number 67 didn't quite survive long enough to carry its new allotted number of 11, even though it was in the course of preparation when it was sold to W. North of Leeds. One interesting aspect concerning this contract was that the revised order, placed in February 1946, was initially for 8ft wide buses but this was later changed to the more usual width at the time of 7ft 6ins, due to a combination of delivery delays and route restrictions where Traffic Commissioners' approval was required to operate 8ft wide buses on specific routes. In the event Preston never operated any 8ft wide PD1s or PD2s.

Service improvements were resumed on 11th November 1946 when the Ashton services were re-organised. Basically, the Ashton Lane Ends A was re-lettered B and denoted on bus blinds as Ashton Inkerman Street. It was also altered to return from Lane Ends to Central Station via the same route as that used outward. The previous Ashton Lane Ends B service was re-lettered D and altered to run from the Town Centre via Central Station to Lane Ends before returning to town as service C, via Brook Street. Reciprocally, buses on service C returned from Lane Ends to town as service D. However, through running on services C and D did not last long and the practice was discontinued in April 1947. The C route was later linked to the HS with buses running between the two outer termini via the Town Centre. The following month saw the introduction of a short-lived service to Trafford Street, lettered TS. One unusual aspect of this service is that it has been the only Corporation stage service ever to have operated along Moor Lane, which is quite surprising since the latter is one of the main roads in the central area of the town.

Nineteen-hundred and forty-seven brought the delivery of a further 21 Leyland PD1As. The 'A' in the chassis designation indicated that Metalastik rubber bushes were fitted in the spring shackle pins, instead of metal bushes. In April Nos. 71-3, 90-4 (BCK621-8) were received from Leyland, whilst in October highbridge examples 95-102 (BCK629-36) and lowheight examples 103-7 (BCK936-40), completed the orders. Whilst these were again fitted with Leyland style bodies Nos. 95-100 had in fact been sub-contracted out to nearby Samlesbury Engineering Ltd for assembly. Seating was the same as the earlier batches.

Modernisation of the fleet began in 1946 with the purchase of ten Leyland PD1s. No. 88, seen here in Birley Street in the mid-'fifties, was one of a batch of seven highbridge models bodied by Walter Alexander to Leyland's Design.

(Author's collection)

Top: 1946 Alexander bodied Leyland PD1 No. 84, as originally built, is pictured on the Queens Drive PL stand in Birley Street in the early 'fifties. Thirty-one PD1As were introduced to the fleet in the years 1946/7 which were mainly used to expand the existing services.

(R. Marshall)

Centre: Three PD1s with lowheight bodies, Nos. 60/6/7, were bought in 1946 specifically to work on the Pedders Lane Ashton A service. This view shows No. 67 outside the Harris Library in Birley Street. A further five lowheight PD1As, Nos. 103-7, entered the fleet the following year.

(R. Marshall)

Right: Lowheight Leyland PD1 No. 66 is parked up in Deepdale Road with an unidentified PD2/1 behind on Football Special duty in the mid-'fifties. The football stand just visible in the background, which was one of the oldest in the football league, was demolished in 1995 to make way for a new futuristic all-seater stand.

(R. Marshall)

No. 64 was the last of the trio (62-4) of 1936 English Electric-bodied Leyland TD4cs to remain in service, being withdrawn in 1957. This view shows No. 64 in Harris Street on the Ashton Lane Ends stand sometime in the 1950s by which time sliding window openers had replaced its original half-drop variety and it had gained a single piece destination screen.

(R. Marshall)

A late 1950s view of 1947 Leyland PD1A No. 73 at the Lane Ends stand in Harris Street which for many years was the author's local bus route. This was one of the buses which was converted for use as a mobile polling station in August 1964.

(Author's collection)

Below: Seen in the garage yard in its guise as a recovery vehicle is former 1947 Leyland PD1A ex bus No. 106 (6), in the company of PD2/1 115. No. 106 was converted for use as a breakdown vehicle following an accident in May 1960 and it was used as such between 1962 & 1978.

(P. Hesketh collection)

30

In this view Leyland TD4c No. 16, still wearing the three cream bands livery, is pictured in front of the Harris Library in Birley Street. No. 16, along with 32, was one of the last of the large batch of tramway replacement vehicles to remain in service, eventually being withdrawn in 1957.

(S. N. J. White)

Of the lowheight batch 106 was renumbered to 6 in April 1957 and it is also thought that 107 carried its new allotted number 7 for a short while before its withdrawal in 1958. Numbers 103-5 were to have been renumbered to 3, 4, and 1 respectively, but events overtook the intention and the vehicles were withdrawn before the scheme could be fully implemented. Number 6 (BCK939) was badly damaged in an accident involving a low bridge (the Danger Bridge) in May 1960 and the author has vivid memories of seeing the incumbent vehicle firmly wedged underneath the bridge. It was subsequently cut down and rebuilt as a recovery vehicle; in addition, sometime after 1970, it also acquired an O.600 engine. It was used as such from circa December 1962 until March 1978. Fortunately the PD1 recovery vehicle still exists today in preservation. All the foregoing vehicles were bought mainly for fleet expansion and whilst no new buses were bought in 1948 only six, five TDs and a solitary Lion, had succumbed by the end of 1949. Of these, TD4 No. 31 was the first of the large batch of tramway replacement buses bought in 1935 to go, in 1947. Having completed only twelve years of service it is possible that body failure was the cause of its early demise since no more of the batch were withdrawn until 1950 and the last in service, Nos. 16 and 32, lasted ten years longer than No. 31.

Throughout the year discussions had been held with Ribble Motor Services (including Scout Motor Services) regarding joint operating arrangements within the Borough. Eventually an agreement was reached whereby future new services which operated to developing areas immediately outside the Borough boundary would be jointly operated and Ribble would not set down passengers going out of town or pick up passengers coming into town on their own services, within the Borough, other than on the jointly operated services. From 1st January 1948 the agreement came into force and a new series of route numbers was introduced to denote the 'jointly operated' services; these being P1

etc. The P1 service was a combination of the Frenchwood FR and the Ashton D which was then extended via Long Lane and Blackpool Road to Lea (Victoria Park Drive). Through running from Frenchwood to Lea via the Town Centre was therefore introduced and Ribble generally provided one of the seven buses required to operate the normal Mon-Sat daytime schedules. The P2 and P4 were interworked services from Lightfoot Lane (Fulwood) to the Plough Inn and Crookings Lane respectively at Penwortham, again operating via the Town Centre. The P4 was very short lived and lasted exactly four months before being withdrawn, with all journeys henceforth running through to the Plough as P2. Finally in the 'P' group of routes was the P5, which ran from Ribbleton Gamull Lane to the Anchor Inn at Hutton and traversed Ribbleton Avenue, Ribbleton Lane and Church Street to the Town Centre and then on via Fishergate and Liverpool Road to Hutton. Initially the P2, P4 and P5 were worked by a combination of Ribble and Corporation vehicles but by December 1948 arrangements had been made whereby principally only Ribble vehicles worked on the P2 and Corporation vehicles worked on the P5, although extras were sometimes provided by the other operator. These new routes took Corporation buses outside the Borough boundary on a regular basis for the first time. Other alterations which took place at this time included the withdrawal of the Ashton Lane Ends D, replaced by the new P1, and the introduction of a new service to Ribbleton Gamull Lane from the Town Centre. This latter service was an extension of the service to Chatburn Road which was relettered from R to GL and the timetable was fully interworked with buses running through from Hutton on the new jointly operated P5. In consequence of the letters GL being adopted for the new service the existing Gamull Lane route, which operated via Deepdale Road and Watling Street Road, was relettered to FR for Fulwood Row, which joined Watling Street Road at the same junction as Gamull Lane.

Above: This quiet mid-'fifties scene in the town centre depicts 1947 lowheight Leyland PD1A No. 105, which is turning out of Birley Street alongside the old Town Hall.

(C. Carter)

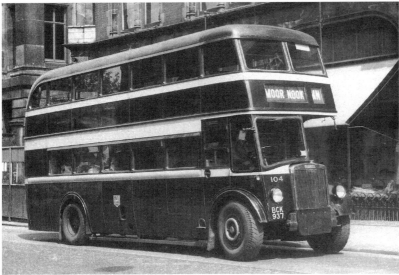

Left: Number 104 was another of the five lowheight PD1As which were bought in 1947 for the Ashton A service. In this early 1950s view taken alongside Miller Arcade in Birley Street it is seen, somewhat unusually, employed on the Moor Nook route.

(R. Marshall)

Below left: No. 92, one of a batch of eight PD1As numbered 71-3, 90-4 which were introduced in 1947, is seen here in original condition outside the Transport Offices in Lancaster Road sometime in the early 'fifties. It was also one of the last PD1s to remain in service being replaced by the first Panthers in December 1968.

(R. Marshall)

Whilst there were no new vehicle acquisitions in 1948, the following year a pair of Leyland Tiger PS1s, Nos. 74/5 (CRN79, 80), the single-deck equivalent of the PD1, were bought to replace Lions Nos. 76 and 77; the two Tiger chassis were in actual fact constructed in 1946 but due to wartime restrictions they had to be stored for some time before bodying could take place.

Numbers 74/5 had 35 seat bodies built by the Yorkshire Yacht Building Co, a small firm in Bridlington, on behalf of East Lancashire Coachbuilders with whom the order had originally been placed. In 1950 East Lancs took control of the YY Co but after the firm

Above: Looking immaculately turned out is 1951 PD1 No. 127 waiting on the PL stand in Birley Street. This particular bus was a somewhat elusive vehicle since it tended to spend more time in use as a driver trainer whilst still being licensed as a psv.

(Senior Transport Archive)

Right: One of a pair of Leyland PS1s purchased in 1949, No. 74 carried a 35 seat YYC/East Lancs body. Seen here on Private Hire duty in the 'fifties it was withdrawn in December 1968 but then saw further use with the Corporation in the early 'seventies as a mobile polling station.

(R. Marshall)

had gone into voluntary liquidation in 1952 activities were concentrated on Blackburn. East Lancs was a firm not previously used by Preston and one which was not to figure in any more purchases for a further 27 years. The fleet strength at the close of the decade was 101 and although this was a high point the size of the fleet then remained remarkably constant right through to 1979.

In 1947 Leyland had introduced the O.600 engine which was equivalent to 9.8 litres in capacity and it was proved in many fleets to be capable of running for longer periods between overhauls. The O.600 engine remained in production right up until 1972 and was therefore used to power all subsequent Titans purchased by Preston.

From August 1950 the Ultimate ticket machine was preferred to the TIMs and these held sway for many years, even surviving right through the 'PAYB' conversion era. At the Transport Committee meeting held on 18th September it was resolved to apply to the Traffic Commissioners to operate buses to the Continuation Hospital in Longsands Lane and at the following meeting, in November, a further resolution was made to seek permission to run buses to Sharoe Green Hospital. Just over twelve months later buses started serving the Continuation Hospital on various days of the week by the diversion of certain journeys on the FR service. By March 1954 a separate service was being run from town to the Hospital and this continued without alteration, other than the days and times of operation, right up until its closure in June 1984. The initial service to Sharoe Green Hospital was a modest affair with a bus being provided in early 1952 to run the short distance from Watling Street Road to the Hospital entrance in Sharoe Green Lane. This service was withdrawn after a three month trial period, but the following year a single Sunday morning journey was introduced to run from the Depot via Farringdon Park and the Town Centre. Operation ceased after 11th April 1981, by which time the service had become WSO.

Replacement of the pre-war fleet began in earnest at the start of the decade. Between December 1950 and February 1951 20 new 56-seat Leyland bodied PD2/1s, with vacuum brakes, were received from the Farington Works and were numbered 108-27 (DRN291-310). Somewhat unusually for the Leyland body they had flush mounted rubber glazed windows and separately mounted sliding openers. This method of construction was first used by Leyland in October 1948 on a PD2/3 built for Bloemfontein Municipality in South Africa. This style of body was commonly known as the Farington-type, the name being taken from the location of Leyland's works. In addition to the revised glazing the traditional style of waistrail moulding was eliminated and this was probably a deciding factor in the move away from the three cream band livery as this became somewhat difficult to achieve within the bodyside beadings. Various other vehicles in the fleet at this time also had similar mounted windows to varying degrees, acquired when modifications had been made to the bodywork over the

Top: In this view 1951 Leyland PD2/1 No. 113 sports its second livery variation (originally the upper deck window surrounds were also cream) and is seen in Lancaster Road, complete with 'Guinness' advert on the front.

(R. Marshall)

Lower: Lowheight PD2/10 No. 5, one of a pair new in 1952, is seen in Birley Street on the service for which it was specifically obtained. No. 5 was withdrawn in 1959 and subsequently rebuilt to PD3 specifications.

(Author's collection)

years. Adverts were first applied to the in-between decks panels on Preston's double-deck buses from sometime in 1952 but in addition one advert which was peculiar to most, if not all of this first batch of PD2s, was a strip advert on the front of the buses, positioned above the destination/route letter screens; most if not all of which read **'Had your Guinness today ?'**. In consequence of this large intake of new vehicles 24 Leyland TDs were withdrawn, which included all the remaining TD2s comprising Nos. 41-50/3, 68-70 and the ex-demonstrator, No. 61 (TJ3278).

Above: This 'fifties scene depicts 1952 PD2/10 No. 42 turning out of Cheapside into Fishergate whilst working the jointly operated service from Hutton to Ribbleton.

(Senior Transport Archive)

Right: Leyland PD2/10 No. 44, new in 1952, and wearing the drab late '50s/early 1960s maroon and single cream band livery waits outside the English Electric Co Works in Strand Road. At one time buses departed to all districts of the town at the end of the afternoon shift. Now sadly the building has been demolished.

(Author's collection)

Right: Number 75 was the second of the pair of Leyland Tiger PS1s received in 1949 from YYC/East Lancashire Coachbuilders. They were somewhat under used buses having little regular work after 1954 but they did find gainful employment between 1964 and 1968 on the free bus service to Fames' supermarket in Dundonald Street. This July 1965 view shows No. 75 in Lancaster Road waiting for prospective shoppers.

(P. J. Relf)

In 1952 more Leyland bodied PD2s were received in the form of lowheight examples Nos. 2 and 5 (ECK509/10) and similar highbridge vehicles Nos. 41-8 (ECK501-8). These were of the PD2/10 marque and at 27ft in length were 1ft longer than the PD2/1s with, in the case of the highbridge models, two extra seats on the lower deck. In 1959 three more seats were added, two upstairs and one down, making them of H32/29R configuration. This followed a resolution made at the Transport Committee meeting held on 21st May 1958, which stated that all buses under five years of age were to have their seating capacities increased by up to a maximum of four, depending on the body style of the vehicles concerned. All buses treated, however, gained a full-width seat for five passengers in the downstairs saloon, immediately behind the bulkhead, which faced towards the back of the bus. Needless to say further TDs were withdrawn together with Leyland Lions Nos. 78/9 and 83. The remaining pre-war single-deckers, Lions Nos. 81/2 and the solitary Tiger No. 80, soldiered on until 1954. Between 1954 and 1968 Preston's single-deck fleet consisted solely of the two 1949 Tigers, Nos. 74/5, and these latterly found employment on the free bus service to Fame's stores in Dundonald Street which commenced operation on 11th December 1964. They even survived long enough to be repainted into the later-adopted blue and ivory livery which looked very smart on these under-used buses. Fame's store finished up as part of the ASDA chain and latterly PD3s were used on the service which ran for the last time on 28th October 1978.

In March 1954 another batch of ten PD2/10s was put into service, again comprising two lowheight and eight highbridge models. The lowheight buses became Nos. 9 and 10 whilst the remainder were haphazardly numbered 49-51/3/4/7/9 and 61, but all were consecutively registered as FRN731-40. For many years Preston generally used the gap filling principle when numbering new buses (and indeed some of the trams) and it wasn't until 1968 that this policy was revised. Whilst six of these buses, together with two of the earlier batch, later became the subject of an ambitious rebuilding programme the remaining four, Nos. 49, 53/4/7, went on to give sterling service with the former bringing the curtain down on the type in March 1976 after having completed 22 years of unbroken service. Even then the story was not complete since 54 and 57 were used as driver tuition vehicles from January 1976 until March 1980. Again all the highbridge examples were upseated by three in 1958/9. As well as the single-deckers previously mentioned additional vehicle withdrawals comprised a handful of TDs which included No. 3, the last but one 1934 TD3, and TD4s Nos. 12/3 and 21.

After the activity of the late 'forties the 1950s were a relatively quiet period for service developments. March 1952 had seen the introduction of a new SO route running to Moor Nook direct via Ribbleton Lane and Ribbleton Avenue, which was lettered M. Consequently the Moorside service had been re-lettered from M to MN and was also shown as Moor Nook on bus destination

Lowheight Leyland PD2/10 No. 9, one of a pair which entered service in 1954, is seen when still fairly new on the Pedders Lane stand in Birley Street.

(S. E. Letts)

This early '60s view, taken in Lancaster Road, shows 1954 PD2/ 10 No. 59 setting out for Broadgate. No. 59 later became the last PD2 to be rebuilt as a PD3/6, re-entering service as such in 1967.

(Author's Collection)

Right: This garage interior view taken circa 1956 shows PD1s Nos. 96, 89, 52 and 104 together with PD2/10 No. 49. No. 89 is recently outshopped in the single cream band livery which replaced that worn by the other buses in this view.

(J. Watson collection)

Below: A 1951 Leyland PD2/1 No. 123 stands outside the Discount Book Company shop (sadly missed by countless bus and train enthusiasts) in Church Street whilst working the PL service in the early 'sixties. This was one of only five PD2/1s which later received the blue and ivory livery.

(Author's collection)

This early 'sixties view shows MCW bodied Leyland PD2/10 No. 83 waiting at the Farringdon Park terminus in Farringdon Crescent (the terminus is now on the opposite side of New Hall Lane in Tudor Avenue). At the time the FP service worked beyond the town centre to either Boys Lane or Queens Drive and it was normal practice to show the ultimate destination throughout.
(R. F. Mack)

This excellent view of 1955 MCW bodied Leyland PD2/10 No. 80, seen departing the Bus Station in 1972, clearly shows the classic lines of MCW's bus bodywork which was synonymous with the 1950s and '60s. Note the black lines which separate the blue and ivory interfaces.

(John Fozard)

blinds. However the new M service did not last long and had been withdrawn by 1958. Another significant route alteration in the 'fifties was the rerouting of the Ashton B away from the 'Danger Bridge', in March 1954, thereby eliminating the need for single-deck buses to operate this service. At this time a large housing estate was being built in the west of the town at Larches, adjacent to Blackpool Road, and following the initial diversion of a few P1 Lea journeys into the estate for the benefit of the workmen engaged on the building work, a full service was established on 4th April 1955 by re-routing alternate buses on the P1 to turn at the junction of Larches Lane and Greaves Town Lane. At the same time journeys on the P1 service to Lea were extended to run further along Blackpool Road to Aldfield Avenue, turning back at the junction of Dodney Drive and then running via Greenside Avenue and Tudor Avenue back to Blackpool Road. Why the opportunity was not taken to renumber the Larches buses remains a mystery, but

then Preston had always had a complicated route numbering system.

Another area of Preston which was rapidly developing was Brookfield, and another Saturdays Only service, lettered CR had been started at the same time as the M to serve the Cromwell Road area. It initially commenced running as a circular service via Ribbleton Lane, Ribbleton Avenue and Cromwell Road to Watling Street Road and then returning via Deepdale Road but later it was altered to an out-and-back route running along Cromwell Road as far as Dunsop Road. By 1958 a pattern of services had been established to Brookfield consisting of :- the BF (introduced 24th July 1958), which ran via Deepdale Road to Croasdale Avenue; the CR, which ran via Cromwell Road and had by then also been extended to Croasdale Avenue; the FR, which had been re-routed from St. Paul's Road to run direct via Deepdale Road following the same route as the BF but terminating at Fulwood Row; and finally the LS, which

1956 Crossley bodied PD2/10 No. 28 is seen at the junction of Harris Street and Lancaster Road working on the jointly operated service from Hutton to Ribbleton.

(D. Savage)

Crossley bodied Leyland PD2/10 No. 20, new in April 1957 and one of eighteen similar vehicles, sets off for Farringdon Park in this early 'sixties view taken at the top of Church Street at its junction with Lancaster Road.

(Author's collection)

was effectively formed of buses on the FR route extended to Longsands Lane.

Meanwhile the years 1955-7 had seen the introduction of more Leyland PD2/10s, but since Leyland had ceased to build bus bodies other bodybuilding contractors had to be used. In November 1955 a batch of five, Nos. 79-83 (HRN485-9), was received from Metro-Cammell Weymann of Birmingham, which had 58-seat highbridge bodies. One prominent feature of all the PD2/10s was a twin chrome bumper on the back but they were all removed early in the vehicles' operating lives. Amazingly the whole batch of MCWs survived in service for some 21 years, all being withdrawn in 1976, with No. 83 having the distinction (along with Crossley 31) of being one of the last two PD2s in service. On a personal note the MCW batch was always the author's favourite and many journeys were made on them, since they were frequently employed on local services to Lane Ends (C), Larches / Lea (P1/P3) and later, Ingol (P4).

One particular quirk of the type gave rise to the name of 'Marbles Buses' since the rivet heads trapped between the outer and inner skins of the roof lining had the tendency to slide from side to side when the buses negotiated one of the many 90° bends on the local routes. In common with the previous batches of PD2s they were upseated in 1962 with the addition of one upper and three lower deck seats, making them of H33/29R configuration. Alas none of the batch was saved for preservation and the author well remembers Nos. 80-3 looking forlorn in the complex of Barnsley breakers' yards in April 1977. Number 79 did in fact survive longer, having been purchased by a Promotions concern in 1976 and was last recorded in use in 1983.

A further 18 Leyland PD2/10s were bodied by the Stockport firm of Crossley in 1956/7. Crossley was a member of the ACV Group which included Park Royal Vehicles Ltd. of London. These were the first buses to have heaters of the Clayton Dewandre type installed

This 1960s view shows 1957 Crossley bodied PD2/10 No. 36 laying over in Lancaster Road. The Ribble Offices, just visible behind, were the first of a line of buildings leading towards the left of the picture which was demolished to make way for the Guild Hall which was opened in 1972.

(Author's collection)

Seen in Birley Street when still fairly new is 1958 MCW bodied Leyland PD3/5 No. 63. Even though they were regular performers on the BR/MN services, 8ft wide buses initially caused problems on the Moor Nook route, due to the narrowness of the carriageways in Cemetery Road and Miller Road.

(Author's collection)

No. 9 (NCK741) was the first of the Preston rebuilds, whereby various lowheight and highbridge Leyland bodied PD2s were rebuilt to a PD3/6 specification. No. 9 is seen in its early days as a PD3 on Fishergate Bridge returning from Broadgate.

(Author's Collection)

from new, other than TD2 No. 61. Numbers 24-8 (JCK583-7) were delivered in July 1956, whilst Nos. 20-3/9-37 (KCK328-30, KRN419-28) were a protracted delivery spread over nine months from April to December 1957. Whilst the 1956 examples were again of H30/28R configuration the remainder were delivered with two extra seats on the upper deck. All later became H32 or H33/29R between 1959 and 1961. The introduction of these buses produced a further simplified livery of all maroon with a single cream band in-between decks which was then applied to all the Titans, both existing and future deliveries. Unlike the MCW batch the withdrawal of the Crossley-bodied PD2s was spread over several years starting with No. 25 in October 1969, following an accident, and not being concluded until No. 31 was withdrawn some seven years later. Fortunately the latter was saved for preservation and still exists in 1995. Numbers 35/7 also saw use as driver tuition vehicles. The same period saw the withdrawal of almost all the remaining pre-war TDs, leaving just the 1939/40 examples active. Fleet modernisation was virtually complete having taken just eleven years to replace virtually all the pre-war buses.

All the post-war deckers, which comprised 31 PD1s and 63 PD2s, had rear entrance open platform bodywork, but all this was to change in 1958 when Preston bought the first of 26 new Leyland PD3s. However, before this came about the story reverts to 1955. In November of that year an order was placed with Leyland Motors for the delivery of seven PD2 chassis which were intended to receive one lowheight and six highbridge bodies, for introduction into service in 1958. It was eventually decided to order bodywork of the 'Beverley Bar' design, which was peculiar to many double-deck buses operated by East Yorkshire Motor Services in order to permit their use under the Bar (Arch) in the town of that name. It was generally thought that these would be suitable to pass under the railway bridge in Fylde Road, which was somewhat restricted in both height and width, and it was intended that they would replace lowheight examples. However other events overtook this interesting proposal when in 1957 the road surface was actually lowered under the offending bridge, thereby permitting normal height buses to pass underneath providing they kept to the centre of the carriageway; a situation which still exists today. This not only led to a further change in the order for the 1958 deliveries but also to a very ambitious rebuilding programme whereby existing lowheight and highbridge buses were extensively rebuilt.

The seven new buses for 1958 eventually emerged as Nos. 62-8 (MCK293-9), which were air braked Leyland PD3/5s fitted with 72 seat Metro-Cammell Weymann-built bodies. These entered service in December of that year and were the first 8ft wide buses employed by Preston, whilst at 30ft in length they also presented one or two problems for the operator when used on certain

MCW bodied Leyland PD3/5 No. 68, new in 1958, is pursued by Crossley bodied PD2/10 No. 20, only 20 months its senior, towards Fishergate Bridge. The Broadgate was an early recipient of 8ft-wide buses whilst the P5 was for many years Preston's longest route, albeit jointly operated with Ribble Motor Services.

(Author's collection)

New in 1961 MCW bodied Leyland PD3/4 No. 17 is seen in the early 'sixties at the Brookfield/Fulwood Row stand in Harris Street. Compare this view of No. 17 with that shown on page 60.

(John Fozard)

Still with a shine on its paintwork 1963 MCW-bodied PD3A/1 No. 90 is seen in Church Street crossing the junction of Lancaster Road pursued by Crossley PD2/10 No. 20.
(Author's collection)

routes with a proliferation of tight corners, notably to Moor Nook (MN), Holme Slack (HS) and Ashton Lane Ends (C). They featured sliding doors and a rear facing staircase, whilst in the lower saloon the seats over the wheel arches were of the longitudinal facing type; Numbers 62-8 did in fact set the trend for the three subsequent batches of MCW / PD3s bought new from the same manufacturers between 1961 and 1965. They were also the first post-war buses built new with a single piece destination/route letter aperture at the front. Several PD1s and non-Leyland bodied PD2s were altered to the same format, having been built with separate destination and route letter apertures. These first PD3s again gave sterling service averaging some 20 years of continual use thereby highlighting the fact that, coupled with proper maintenance procedures, Leyland buses of the era were extremely reliable and robust machines. Also in 1958 the last four TDs, Nos. 38-40 and 65, bowed out

together with the first new post-war buses, lowheight PD1s Nos. 67, 105 and 107 (7).

New vehicle acquisitions tailed off somewhat at this time although interest was maintained with the decision to start a programme of bus rebuilding in March 1959. The Transport Committee first gave approval for work to be done on two buses and since lowheight buses were no longer a requirement, two such examples, PD2s 5 (ECK510) and 9 (FRN731), were selected to be so treated. Number 9 was the first to enter the Corporation's own workshops and over an approximate eight month period it was transformed into a new vehicle of PD3 proportions. Not only was it increased to the full height of 14ft 6ins but it was also extended to 30ft in length and widened to 8ft, with the result being classified as a PD3/6, having an H41/32F body configuration. Some of the tasks involved included the provision of new main and cross members to the chassis, new wider axles and the fitting of stronger springs to carry the extra weight. The opportunity was also taken to install a newly reconditioned O.600 engine. When the chassis assembly had been completed the new lower deck was built on it and then the upper deck was added. The whole project, which is reported to have cost £2,283 (less than half the cost of a new PD3), was considered a resounding success and a credit to the men who had worked on the conversion. Number 9 was registered for service on 1st November 1959. No time was lost in carrying out the second conversion and No. 5 emerged as such in July 1960, looking very similar but with three fewer seats on the upper deck. Both vehicles were re-registered becoming NCK741 (9) and NCK757 (5). It may be felt that eight months for a vehicle conversion is a somewhat protracted period but it must be remembered that this work was done in addition to all the routine bodywork repairs etc. and the vehicles were not worked on continuously.

During the course of 1960 more lowheight PD1s were withdrawn comprising Nos. 60 (8), 66 (12), 103/4, together with the first highbridge example, No. 87. Also in that year the bus replacement policy again threatened to take an unusual turn when it was decided to order five Atlanteans with highbridge bodywork, having seating for 78 passengers. However, mainly due to union resistance, this policy was not pursued and the next new buses were again PD3s. These arrived in 1961 as Nos. 13-19 (PRN905-11) and were again bodied by Metro-Cammell Weymann, but the chassis marque was

the PD3/4 fitted with synchromesh gears instead of the pneumocyclic type fitted to Nos. 62-68 (67 was later converted to a PD3/4). Seating was two fewer than the latter with one less on each deck. Again they survived in service for many years and several of the batch were amongst the last Titans in regular use in 1980. Amazingly only one vehicle went directly for scrap, that being No. 18. At least three still survived in 1994 with No. 14 in preservation, 17 in use by the Undertaking as a Driver Tuition Vehicle and 16, substantially rebuilt, in the guise of a recovery vehicle; the last two however were disposed of by the Company the following year. Numbers 13-19 replaced an equal number of PD1s which comprised Nos. 52, 71, 88-90/9 and 102, all of which passed via W. North of Leeds to the Yorkshire independent, Samuel Ledgard of Armley. The final new PD3s comprised two batches; one formed of seven vehicles, Nos. 84-90 (TRN386-92), in 1963; the other of five, Nos. 69-73 (ARN654-8C), in 1965. All had Metro-Cammell Weymann H39/31F bodies on a Leyland PD3A/1 chassis; the letter 'A' denoting the fibreglass style front grille first seen on buses built for St. Helens Corporation Transport in 1960. The latter batch, delivered between

Seen in the early stages of its conversion to a PD3/6 is 1954 Leyland PD2/10 No. 61 (FRN740), the penultimate rebuild. This conversion was started in 1963 and completed in March 1965 when it re-entered service with the registration BCK367C.

(P. Hesketh collection)

connection with the 1972 Preston Guild.

The early 'sixties were completely devoid of any significant route changes and it was to be early 1965 before any more alterations of any note were effected. On 12th February the Ashton B was withdrawn, having latterly become a Mon-Sat peak hours only operation, and at the same time the Lea service was renumbered to P3 and re-routed to fill the gap on Waterloo Road vacated by the B. Also at this time the first completely new route, since the introduction of the Larches Estate service some ten years previously, started running to a new estate at Ingol in the north of the Borough. Numbered P4 it was a jointly operated service which rather unusually departed from a stand on Ribble's Tithebarn Street Bus Station and even more unusually, due to space problems, it was later relocated onto the Express Coach Station. Initially a very basic timetable was provided but by the following year, 1966, more journeys had been added and the service was extended further into the estate to loop via Barry Avenue, Dunbar Road and Creswell Avenue.

As previously mentioned several PD2s were rebuilt during this period. Although each retained the original fleet number all were re-registered as new buses before entering service, viz No. 2 (PRN761, ex-ECK509) in 1961, 10 (PRN762, ex-FRN732) and 50 (SRN375, ex-FRN734) in 1962, 51 (SRN376, ex-FRN735) in 1963 and 61 (BCK367C, ex-FRN740) in 1965. The final rebuild, bringing the total to eight, was No. 59 (FCK453F,

February and April 1965, were the last new buses to wear the maroon and cream livery. Two of the earlier batch, Nos. 87/8, were painted with cream radiator grilles for a short period in 1966/7, but regrettably (in the author's opinion) this livery modification was not extended to the remainder of the batch. In 1972 No. 88 became the first double-deck bus to be painted in an overall advert colour scheme, this being for Dorman Smith Electrical Switchgear, which was done in

Above: This specially posed photograph shows the four experimental liveries which were tried in 1966/7 prior to changing the fleet colours from maroon/cream to blue/ivory. Depicted here on the Moor are Crossley bodies Nos. 33/5, Leyland body No. 43 and MCW body No. 81, all PD2/10s dating from the 'fifties. No. 35 got the vote of confidence and the rest is now consigned to history.
(Ribble Enthusiasts Club)

Seen in its experimental light blue and white livery, worn in 1966/7, is 1955 MCW bodied PD2/10 No. 81 at the Frenchwood stand in a somewhat deserted Birley Street. The then newly built Crystal House (some twenty years later the author's place of work) in the background, was at the time mainly unoccupied.

(R. F. Mack)

A couple of years after its conversion 1965 PCTD rebuild No. 61 is seen waiting alongside Miller Arcade in Lancaster Road. Withdrawn in March 1978 it was one of four rebuilds which were initially preserved.

(R. F. Mack)

ex-FRN739) which entered service as such in September 1967, resplendent in the then newly-adopted blue and ivory livery. Livery experiments had been carried out in September 1966 when four PD2s were painted in a variety of blue and ivory or cream colour schemes. The vehicles selected were Crossleys 33/5, Leyland 43 and MCW 81. Number 43 was painted mainly Oxford blue with a broad white band applied to the in-between decks panels; No. 81 wore a light blue and white livery in a similar arrangement, whilst Nos. 33/5 received mid-blue and ivory paint schemes. The former was painted mainly ivory with a blue roof and window surrounds and the latter was treated to a similar arrangement with the colours applied in reverse, except the roof which was again blue. Number 35, which the author remembers seeing tucked away in the garage fresh out of the paintshop, was generally considered by employees and the travelling public alike to be the most attractive of the four and its colour scheme was consequently adopted as the new fleet livery. As a further experiment some vehicles, notably PD2s 36, 47 and 82, were painted in a deeper shade of 'cream' known as royal ivory, which had only marginal differences from the previous colour used but it did tend to complement the blue slightly better. The maroon and cream livery finally disappeared in June 1971 with the withdrawal of Crossleys 26/8 which, along with Nos. 25/7 and 30 of the same batch, never received the new colours.

By the middle of 1968 just four PD1s remained in service and the first PD2, No. 110, had been withdrawn following an accident in November 1967. Five of the PD1s withdrawn in 1963, Nos. 72/3, 85/6 and 98, saw further use with the Corporation as mobile polling booths, but all were disused by 1969 and sold for scrap. One PD1, No. 88 (ARN392), has miraculously survived and is now the subject of a long-term restoration project. After seeing several years service in West Yorkshire with Samuel Ledgard, as one of the ex-Preston PD1s acquired by that company in 1961, No. 88 later passed to the Rufforth Gliding Club near York where it languished as a control tower until 1986 before being rescued and brought back to the North West.

In the early 'sixties further alterations were made to the garage, whereby a new covered accommodation shed was constructed to the rear of the existing garage. This work was completed by April 1964 and enabled the whole fleet to be garaged undercover for the first time since before the war. There was no longer any need for the steam heating pipe system and this was consequently dispensed with. The 1960s had generally been a lean time for new acquisitions and certainly towards the latter years of the decade the Transport Department was somewhat hesitant as to which direction to follow for future bus purchases.

Above right: 1957 Crossley bodied PD2/10 No. 33 sports an experimental ivory/blue colour scheme in this 1967 view taken outside Crystal House at the top of Fishergate, formerly the site of the fire ravaged Town Hall.
(R. F. Mack)

Right: Crossley bodied Leyland PD2/10 No. 35 was the first bus painted in the subsequently adopted blue/ivory livery. This view of No. 35 was taken in Lancaster Road, circa 1967. At least the dry cleaners appears to be doing a good trade.
(Author's collection)

4. FROM CREW TO ' PAYB ' OPERATION

(1968-1986)

At the Transport Committee meeting held on 18th October 1965 a tender from Metro-Cammell Weymann was accepted for the supply of five 70-seat double-deck bus bodies at a cost of £3,525 each to be mounted on Leyland PD3/4 chassis which were then on order. However certain events resulted in a change, not only to this particular order but to the future bus replacement policy in general, which was to last right through to the mid-1970s. In August 1966 a Leyland Panther (CRH173C) was taken on loan from Kingston-upon-Hull City Transport and the performance of this totally different machine was sufficient to convince the Committee that 'One-man' (term of the era before sex equality) operation was the way forward and since legislation did not yet allow one-man-operation on double-deckers this could only mean a return to single-deckers. Consequently five Leyland Panther chassis were ordered instead of further PD3 examples, but the body building contract remained with MCW. The Leyland Panther had its engine mounted behind the rear axle, but with a front radiator, thereby requiring long pipes

to carry the coolant from the front to the back and the chassis had a very low frame which stepped up immediately ahead of the rear axle. In 1968 five Panther chassis were stored for a while inside the garage awaiting call up by the body builder and the first completed vehicle (No. 201) was received from MCW towards the end of June with the remainder, 202-5, having been taken into stock by October. These vehicles started a trend of matching registration numbers, being registered HCK201-5G. They were dual-doored buses with seats for 47 passengers and room for a further 18 standees.

Above right: In August 1966 Preston borrowed a Leyland Panther from Kingston-upon-Hull City Transport which was used to assess the practicalities of 'one-man operation'. Hull No. 173, new in 1965 with Roe bodywork, has been caught in Lancaster Road working as a crewed vehicle.

(Author's collection)

Right: The first Leyland Panther was No. 201, one of a batch of five bodied by MCW in 1968, which is seen in its original livery application waiting on the Brookfield stand in Birley Street some time in 1969. The Brookfield group of routes was amongst the first to be converted to 'PAYB' operation on 2nd December 1968.

(Author's collection)

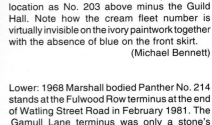

Left: Photographed in March 1981, only a matter of a few weeks before its demise, 1968 MCW bodied Panther No. 203 picks up passengers in Lancaster Road on the erstwhile Frenchwood service. The Guild Hall is the prominent building in the background.

Centre: In this July 1969 view Marshall bodied Panther No. 210 is seen in exactly the same location as No. 203 above minus the Guild Hall. Note how the cream fleet number is virtually invisible on the ivory paintwork together with the absence of blue on the front skirt.
(Michael Bennett)

Lower: 1968 Marshall bodied Panther No. 214 stands at the Fulwood Row terminus at the end of Watling Street Road in February 1981. The Gamull Lane terminus was only a stone's throw away to the right of the picture whereas the road to the left, behind the vehicle, led up to the Longsands Lane terminus.

gently inclined floor which started rising after a step immediately behind the driver's cab area.

In style 201-5 were exactly the same as vehicles being built concurrently as part of a large order for Liverpool Corporation Transport and it seems more than likely that they were actually slotted into the production line. The blue and ivory was applied in an attractive layout which was peculiar only to this batch but on receiving their first full repaint the layout was somewhat modified in line with subsequent batches of Panthers in that the blue was applied uniformly to the roof, skirt and doors only. All the Panthers eventually operated were delivered with the blue to the skirt applied to the back (not 201-5) and sides only and it was only later that this was extended to completely encircle the vehicles.

In February 1967 a further order had been placed for ten more Leyland Panther chassis and shortly afterwards the contract to body these was awarded to Marshall's of Cambridge. The completed buses were delivered as Nos. 206-15 (HCK206-15G), in November 1968, and were again of two door configuration with seating for 47. Once driver familiarisation had been completed, and various difficulties with the unions concerning their introduction into service had been ironed out, all fifteen entered regular revenue earning service as 'One man' buses on 2nd December 1968 when a group of routes was converted to 'PAYB' operation. The services concerned were the Broadgate (BR); the Brookfield group (BF, CR, FR and

The latter were all accommodated in the front section of the saloon, with the floor of the back section being stepped up immediately after the centre exit doors. The design of MCW's bodywork clearly reflected this step with a similar change to the waistline and bottom window levels on the outside of the vehicle. Subsequent batches of Panthers had smoother outside lines with a

Right: Seen leaving the Bus Station circa 1973 is Preston PD3/6 rebuild No. 10, formerly PD2/10 FRN732. The battered front dome was somewhat unusual for a Preston bus since they were normally very well turned out.
(Author's collection)

Below right: 1947-built Leyland PD1A No. 97 was one of a batch of six (95-100) subcontracted out to Samlesbury Engineering Ltd for assembly. It is seen here in Birley Street on the Holme Slack stand in January 1962. No. 97 lasted until June 1968, when it was sold to a breaker's yard
(Author's collection)

LS); and the Fulwood and Deepdale circulars (F and D). However, Preston's buses were to continue to see the use of conductors for well over another thirteen years. Numbers 201-15 replaced an equal number of older buses which comprised the last five PD1s Nos. 91-4/7, although the latter had in fact been out of use since June; the two 1949 Tigers, Nos. 74/5, and the first normal PD2 withdrawals which consisted of Nos. 108/11-5/21/7. Number 127 had in effect seen more use as a driver tuition vehicle than as a psv and it was fitted from new with an opening sliding window behind the driver to enable the instructor to communicate with the learner driver. Whilst all the double-deckers appear to have been scrapped both the Tigers survived into preservation. Number 74 was used throughout the 1970s as a mobile polling booth before eventually passing to St. Margaret's High School Transport Society in Aigburth, Liverpool. Following extensive restoration work by the Society it returned to Preston in September 1983 where it was painted back into the original maroon and cream livery in the Department's own workshops.

The other significant event towards the close of the 1960s was the opening of the new 'Central' Bus Station, on 12th October 1969, which was built on land adjoining Tithebarn Street. Some of the land had already been vacant for some years and indeed the Corporation actually used to park a few spare buses during the daytime in an area known as Spring Gardens. However, buildings which did give way to the new development included the old Fire Station (which had already been replaced) and Ribble's Express Coach Station. The locality is now unrecognisable from the early 'sixties with only the Tithebarn Public House left to give any clues as to the early geography of the area. Overnight all the Corporation's services were transferred away from the Town Centre on-street bus stands to the new Bus Station, using departure gates numbered between 1 and 40. Meanwhile all other operators, notably Ribble and the Leyland independent, J. Fishwick & Sons, were allocated gate numbers between 41 and 80, which were situated on the opposite side of the central island. All the characteristic pre-war bus shelters dotted about the town centre were quickly removed and now all trace of the original bus stands has disappeared, the last remnants having been removed in the late 'eighties by pedestrianisation works. At the time of opening the new Bus Station was the largest in Europe and was, and still is, a very impressive structure with car parking spaces for some 1200 cars also provided on the nine split floor levels above the central concourse.

Further batches of new dual-door Panthers were received in each of the years 1970-2. In 1970 seven more

Marshall bodied examples were taken into stock and given fleet numbers 216-22 (KRN216-22H), whilst in 1971 the first of two batches with Seddon Pennine bodywork entered service carrying numbers 223-9 (MCK223-9J). The Marshall bodied examples had seating for 49 whilst the Seddons had just one less but were licensed for 21 standees (as opposed to eighteen for the MCWs and Marshalls). In addition, in November 1971, Preston acquired five 'third-hand' Panthers with Marshall B41D Camair bodies. These had been new to Stratford-upon-Avon Blue Motors Ltd in 1970 as their numbers 31-5, registered XNX131-5H, but at the time the Ministry of Transport refused to accept their type of centre exit doors and they passed unused with that undertaking to Midland Red which painted them red and re-registered them as AUE309-13J, giving them fleet numbers 2031-3/5 (34 never received its 20xx number since it was at Preston at the time for demonstration purposes during which time it was actually fitted with a Leyland National engine !). Midland Red didn't use them either and they eventually entered

service with Preston as Nos. 230-4. The body style did not incorporate side destination boxes, unlike all the other Panthers bought new, and the peculiar centre exit doors tended to be slow in closing resulting in their use mainly on generously timed routes. In July 1972 the batch was renumbered to 237-41 to make way for the final batch of new Panthers which were given fleet numbers 230-6 and registered RTF430-6L. The 'Camairs' were later rebuilt, in 1980, when they acquired six extra seats, made possible by the removal of a somewhat generously large luggage pen. At the same time the exit doors were changed to the more conventional type used on Atlanteans thereby improving their boarding time at bus stops. Also at this time Preston acquired a withdrawn Panther from Manchester City Transport for use as a source of spares. The vehicle concerned was GND94E and the body was scrapped immediately whilst the chassis was systematically dismantled over a number of years for its reusable parts.

Returning to Nos. 230-6, these were the final Panthers taken into stock and again had 48-seat Seddon Pennine bodies entering service in August 1972, except for No. 236 that is. This last bus was first seen in public in the 1972 Guild Trades Procession in September but it did not actually enter revenue earning service until early 1973; the reason being that it was initially experimentally fitted with CAV (fully automatic) transmission and first underwent various tests in this guise. Further fame befell 236 in October 1982 when it was selected to carry the Red Rose Rambler bus ticket promotion colour scheme; the only single-decker bus from the various

participating Lancashire bus fleets to do so. It was still in this livery when withdrawn in August 1984. Booked registrations for the batch had been NRN230-6K but although these were briefly carried they were cancelled at the last moment due to their late entry into service. Finally 233/5/6 were renumbered to 33/5/6 in October 1983 simply to eliminate such high fleet numbers from the fleet. Always mindful to improve maintenance access to their vehicles, something which the manufacturers did not always take sufficiently into account, the bodybuilders rebuilt the back-ends of all the Panthers, except 201-7/9/11/5, whereby a much more practical arrangement of hinged panels was provided so that the engine and other components could be made more easily accessible.

As more Panthers entered service in the early 'seventies so more services were converted to PAYB operation which included the service to Moor Nook, MN. When 8ft wide buses, viz the PD3s, had first been introduced to the MN service difficulties were experienced when vehicles passed each other in the Cemetery Road/Miller Road vicinity due to the narrowness of the carriageways and consequently buses travelling out of town had been re-routed onto Acregate Lane, instead of Skeffington Road. History repeated itself when the Panthers were introduced, with the problem this time being the additional length of the vehicles, and consequently buses travelling out of town were again rerouted, this time to use Blackpool Road instead of Acregate Lane. By the end of 1972 the full complement of 41 Panthers was in traffic, operating all

stage services, except the FP, GL, HS, PL, P4 and P5, daily and the A, C and MN on Sundays. Apart from the P4 the remaining crewed services all essentially required high capacity vehicles operating to high frequency timetables and single-deckers would have been most unsuitable. Consequently, no more conversions to PAYB operation took place until suitable vehicles had been obtained.

In 1973, a year in which no new buses were received, the fleet size still stood at 95 which meant that a total of 39 Titans along with the two Tigers had been replaced by the Panthers. Further withdrawals from 1969 had included the remaining PD2/1s, of which Nos. 122-6 had survived long enough to carry the blue and ivory livery whilst No. 116, which had first passed to Geof Lister at Bolton before seeing some use with the Ingleton Caving Club, was later reported as having been abandoned in Turkey sometime after 1975. Also included in this tranche of withdrawals were the first of the Crossleys, Nos. 25-8, 30/5/7 and the entire batch of 1952 highbridge PD2/10s, Nos. 41-8. Of the

Road. From 1st October Preston's travelling public was introduced to the unpopular concept of '*correct fare only*', on which services (D and F) the driver did not give change. Fare boxes were installed in six Panthers and passengers were required to insert the correct change into the box under the watchful eye of the driver who would then issue a ticket in the normal way. Under this method the driver did not handle any money with the boxes being emptied at least once a day at the Bus Station or in the case of late buses at the Depot. It was also argued that boarding times had been improved since the driver did not have to spend time rooting in his bag for change. Initially the system was tried as an experiment and was confined solely to the two Fulwood circular routes but despite initial passenger resistance the concept was eventually adopted for all PAYB routes and the remainder of such services were converted from 15th February 1976. On 12th November 1973 the first of two more jointly operated services started running, numbered P6, which was routed to terminate at Ingol Redcar Avenue whilst the following year, on 14th October, the P7 started running to Savick Luton Road. Both routes were initially crew operated and provided only an infrequent Mon-Fri service with Preston providing buses for all the journeys on the P7 and both operators providing an equal number of buses on the P6. The P7 later gained a Saturday timetable.

With the change in attitude at national level towards the use of double-deckers on PAYB routes and the subsequent availability of government grants towards the purchase of such vehicles, Preston reverted in 1972 to a policy of buying double-deck vehicles. In April that year an Alexander bodied Atlantean, XKC831K, was taken on loan from Merseyside PTE for an assessment of the type. The Atlantean's performance was compared with that of the Leyland National of which two demonstrator examples, DAO851K and FRM499K, were provided by Leyland Motors. The Atlantean must

aforementioned two found further use as driver tuition vehicles, with 125 being used as such between April 1973 and October 1975 and 43 performing similar duties from January 1972 through to November 1974, during which time the latter lost all the glazing to its upper deck windows. In such a state it was finally bought for scrap by one of the Barnsley group of breakers in April 1975.

Substantial reroutings to services in the town centre were implemented in both 1972 and 1973 which had included the introduction of a contraflow bus lane in Friargate. In September 1973 the Brookfield via Cromwell Road CR service was reinstated following a three year suspension due to a weight restriction having been placed on the railway overbridge in Cromwell

1958 MCW bodied Leyland PD3/5 No. 62 catches the early morning sun in this late 'sixties view as it leaves the Moor Nook stand in front of Miller Arcade. This is one junction which, against the trend, is no longer controlled by traffic signals. The MN service was amongst the first services which were converted to 'PAYB' in December 1968.

(M. Bennett)

Last of the 1952 highbridge PD2/10s, No. 48, is seen in Jacson Street in the summer of 1967, sporting the recently introduced blue/ivory colours. The conductor has failed to change the route letter blind to HS, following its run to Ashton Lane Ends and back. The whole ECK batch of PD2s was withdrawn in 1971 as more Panthers entered service.

(R. F. Mack)

Below: 1951-built Leyland PD2/1 No. 116 is seen crossing Ringway in July 1969 heading for the Bus Station. Withdrawn in April 1970 116 reportedly ended its days in Turkey.

(R. F. Mack)

Above: No. 222 was the last of the batch of seven Marshall bodied Panthers received in the Spring of 1970. It is seen here in Woodplumpton Road in July 1981 on the infrequent jointly operated service 43 returning from Ingol to town. Service 43 was the last jointly operated service remaining as such until bus de-regulation in October 1986.

have made a more favourable impression since in March 1973 the Transport Committee recommended the acceptance of tenders for ten Atlantean chassis from Leyland and ten high capacity dual-door bodies from Walter Alexander of Falkirk. The type of bodywork chosen was the 'AL' type which was basically of five bay construction using aluminium alloy incorporating equal depth windows on both decks. In choosing this style of bodywork there is evidence to suggest that Preston was somewhat influenced by the similar (but shorter) vehicles then being operated by Southport Corporation. The batch of completed buses was numbered 101-10 (GBV101-10N) and they entered service between December 1974 and February 1975. The seating capacity was eighty-two, split 49 on the upper deck and 33 on the lower deck. Livery was the revised arrangement of mainly ivory with blue roof, skirt, doors and in-between decks band first introduced on PD3 No. 5 in November 1973. In addition, reflecting the Local Government changes made from April 1974, '**Borough of Preston**' fleetnames, which now incorporated the coat of arms, were carried on the lower-deck panels approximately midway along the sides of the buses. From September 1981 the fleet name on all double-deckers was relocated to the front upper-deck side panels.

Numbers 101-10 were initially used on PAYB and crewed routes alike and it wasn't until August 1976 that they were specifically used to convert a route to double-deck PAYB operation. Several of this batch suffered front end collision damage and the opportunity was taken to re-style the lower front end. This was done to reduce future maintenance costs and to improve the clearance of the

During the late '70s and early 1980s Preston based its fleet on the dual-doored 33ft. long Atlantean eventually taking 77 of the type with either Alexander or East Lancs bodywork. Seen at the delightfully scenic Longsands Lane terminus in February 1981 is 1975 Alexander bodied Atlantean No. 106, one of six of the batch which later passed to North Western in September 1987. This is now the site of a new proposed link road to the M6.

front overhang since they were prone to catching the carriageway surface at certain locations. Number 104 was the first to be modified in January 1980 whilst 110 was the last, in July 1984. In between Nos. 102/5-7 were also treated. Another affliction which befell these buses was the installation of audio advertising. No. 102 was first fitted with a cartridge player, amplifier and six speakers on the upper deck in February 1976 and following a six week trial period the remaining nine were similarly treated. However the company promoting the enterprise encountered financial difficulties and the use of the equipment ceased towards the end of the year, although all the components remained in situ. Some years later a similar exercise involved some 55 Atlanteans of which the first ten again participated. The vehicles effectively replaced by 101-10 were all Crossley bodied Titans in the form of Nos. 20-4, 32/3/6. December 1975 saw the withdrawal of the first of the four remaining 1954 PD2s, No. 54 (FRN737), which was then converted for use as a driver tuition vehicle and renumbered to TU1. The following month No. 57 (FRN738) was withdrawn from psv use and joined TU1 (54) as a driver trainer, but unlike FRN737, it retained its original fleet number. Both were withdrawn from training use and sold for scrap in March 1980.

For many years school special work had played a prominent part in the Department's operational activities. In November 1975 a new college of further education known as W.R.Tuson College (renamed Preston College in 1990) was opened in Fulwood and by the following January a comprehensive network of special workings had been established which served every district of the town and which still formed a prominent part of such workings 20 years on. In February 1976 the Transport Committee resolved to accept tenders from both East Lancashire Coachbuilders and Walter Alexander for the supply of ten bodies from each to be mounted on Atlantean chassis over a two year period. In the event the Scottish firm were already over-committed and could not promise to meet delivery dates. Consequently the next 20 Atlantean chassis were all fitted with East Lancs bodies. Unfortunately the Lancashire firm, was painfully slow in delivering the initial ten, Nos. 111-20, a problem which also affected subsequent orders from the same firm and not for the first time the original booked registrations had to be surrendered since this batch should have been registered PHG111-20P. In the event they were registered UFV111-20R and the first to enter service was No. 120 on 8th

Alexander No. 103, new in 1975, shows off its classic lines as it rounds the Market Square in August 1981 with the Guild Hall towering above in the background. The box below the destination screen showed 'Pay on entry exact fare only'.

Number 104 was one of six of the 1974/5 batch of Alexander bodied Atlanteans which were rebuilt at the front. This February 1981 view shows No. 104 picking up in Larches Lane on its return to town.

September 1976, whilst the last was 118 on 18th November. Paradoxically this was at a time when new buses were desperately needed and the remaining PD2s were being forced to continue until they literally expired. In the long run 111-20 eclipsed the last three Crossley PD2s, Nos. 29, 31/4, the last Leylands, 49,53/4/7 and the entire batch of MCWs, 79-83, although in actual fact many of these had succumbed to the expiry of their Certificates of Fitness in the preceding months. The second batch of ten Atlanteans maintained the 82-seating capacity but the split was 50/32 as opposed to the 49/33 of the Alexander bodied examples. Two of the batch did not entirely lead quiet lives with Preston. Number 115, besides being chosen to carry the first all-over advert since PD3A 88 in 1972, had the distinction of sporting an unauthorised livery modification for just two days in June 1981 whereby the ivory on the front lower panel was projected into the blue skirt in the form of a Vee. Not content with all this attention 115 was also sent on loan to East Staffordshire District Council in June 1979 in exchange for the loan of one of their Dennis Dominators (FBF129T). Meanwhile No. 112 achieved notoriety in September 1984 when it was in collision with a BR Class 56 locomotive on the ungated railway crossing in Strand Road. Fortunately the bus was empty at the time and the driver escaped serious injury. The locomotive concerned was 56107 which was leaving the dock complex, as it turned out without authority, with a train of empty tankers bound for the Lindsey oil refinery on Humberside.

Also in 1976 Preston received additional new buses in the shape of three Bristol LHS types which were bodied by Duple Coachbuilders of Blackpool and were given fleet numbers 242-4 (PHG242-4P). All three were delivered in May and whilst Nos. 243/4 had ordinary bus seats for 31 passengers 242 was fitted with coach type seats for the same number and was envisaged as being used equally for private hire and stage work; it was later modified to incorporate a small rear luggage boot. All three had lettering across the back advertising their availability for private hire work. These buses also had manual gearboxes and with the introduction of automatic and semi-automatic gears on the Atlanteans their popularity with the drivers gradually diminished. The three Bristols had the distinction of carrying three sets of fleet numbers during their time with Preston, having been renumbered to 342-4 in April 1977 and again to plain 42-4 in

Pictured in appalling weather conditions in July 1981 is East Lancs bodied Atlantean No. 115 waiting in Blackpool Road, Ashton, before returning to the Cemetery. At the time this service used the number 98 and was limited to just one return journey on Mondays to Fridays. Behind is Alexander No. 106 working through to Lea on the erstwhile service 26.

In May 1976 Preston bought three Duple bodied Bristol LHS midibuses for use on housing estate routes. No. 242, the only one of the trio fitted with coach type seats, is seen when only a few months old taking part in the Ribble Enthusiasts' Club rally, at Southport.

(John Fozard)

1977-built East Lancs bodied Atlantean No. 121 heads along St. George's Road, near the junction of Deepdale Road, on its return to town in August 1981. The Holme Slack has long been the preserve of double-deckers although Panthers and Lynxes have appeared from time to time.

Left: This view of 1979 East Lancs bodied Atlantean No. 133, taken in September 1980, gives the impression that the bus has keeled over into a ditch but in actual fact it is waiting alongside the Hospital in Midgery Lane. The schedule for this working allowed for more than 70 minutes layover although on occasions the bus would return to the Depot in-between the out and return trips.

Below left: Number 138 was an East Lancs bodied Atlantean, new in 1979, and is seen in this August 1981 picture in the grounds of Fulwood Leisure Centre waiting to take youngsters back to Farringdon Park. This and a similar service from Lea have since operated on a regular basis during the summer school holidays.

Further batches of virtually identical East Lancs bodied Atlanteans were taken into stock in 1977 as Nos. 121-30 (CRN121-30S) and in 1979 as Nos. 131-40 (NCK131-40T). The former entered service between October 1977 and January 1978 and the latter between March and June 1979, apart from No. 134 which was delivered to Preston on 16th December 1978 and was put into service some two weeks later. During its early months of service it was used as a demonstrator by East Lancashire. The Blackburn firm was again somewhat late in meeting delivery dates and this is borne out by the fact that the withdrawal of old buses overtook the receipt of new ones by some considerable number and by the end of 1978 the fleet size had fallen to 90; not because of any recession of the services provided but simply because the PD3s became time expired with their Certificates of Fitness running out. All of the foregoing, together with six of the 111-20 batch, later found further use with the South Yorkshire bus company Basichour Ltd, trading as Sheffield Omnibus, for whom many were still operating at the time of writing. Since this company initially based its early acquisitions on ex-Preston buses they retained the same livery and subsequently all their buses have been similarly painted.

On 17th April the P2 to Lightfoot Lane was rather strangely converted back from PAYB to crewed operation. This came about with an agreement with Ribble whereby Preston would operate the P2 to Lightfoot Lane exclusively and Ribble would operate that section

October 1983. They were bought specifically for use on new routes serving housing estates where bigger buses would have proved unsuitable. These comprised the CL to Callon Estate and the G to Grange Estate via Moor Nook together with the conversion of the already jointly operated P7 to Savick. However for a few months between the date of their delivery and the introduction/ conversion of these services on 30th August they were put to work on most of the existing services even to the extent of using them on occasions with conductors, a practice to which they were totally unsuited due to their narrow doorways, steep steps and confined gangways. The Callon service was not a success and was withdrawn after only ten months of operation. Also on this date the Ribbleton Gamull Lane GL service was converted to double-deck PAYB operation, the first such service to use double-deckers specifically and at the same time through running to Hutton was discontinued with the P5 remaining crew operated.

Above: This mid-70s view of 1962 PCTD/Leyland PD3/6 rebuild No. 50, set against a very pleasing architectural backdrop, is taken at the P5 terminus opposite the Anchor Inn at Hutton. Preston ceased to serve this destination in April 1978 when Ribble took the route over completely, in exchange for the P2 to Lightfoot Lane.

(J. Watson collection)

Right: Looking immaculately turned out is Seddon bodied Leyland Panther No. 227, new in 1971, standing alongside the West Coast Main Line at the Lightfoot Lane terminus in February 1981. The P2/28 service terminated at this location between November 1977 and June 1983 when it was further extended through to Tanterton.

of the P2 from Town to Penwortham, which was then renumbered P20, and they would also operate the P5 to Hutton Anchor Inn which was similarly renumbered P50. Consequently the crewed buses which had latterly been used on the P5 took over on the P2. The object of this arrangement was to concentrate all Borough of Preston stage services within the borough boundary, as formed with local government reorganisation on 1st April 1974. The 7th August brought the second service conversion to double-deck PAYB operation when the PL lost its crews and at the same time was extended along Black Bull Lane and Sharoe Green Lane to a new turning circle alongside the Royal Preston Hospital. Henceforth buses showed the new destination of Fulwood via Plungington Road vice the previous Queens Drive.

The first PD3 to be taken off the road had been No. 66 in December 1976. Between then and November

1979 a further 21 PD3s were taken out of service. These comprised the remainder of the 1958 MCW bodied batch, although 65 defied attempts to retire the vehicle twice before it finally succumbed in May 1979; two of the similar 1961 vehicles, 16/8; and all eight of the rebuilds together with all but two of the 1963 MCW/ PD3As, of which just 85 and 90 then remained. The latter was the last PD3 to undergo a major overhaul, in October 1978. Of the eight rebuilds, Nos. 9, 10, 50/1 were sold to breakers in the Barnsley area whilst 5, 59 and 61 went for preservation although 59 subsequently also went for scrap. Both this and No. 5 were given full repaints in Preston livery before being collected by their new owner. At the time of writing No. 2 was in the course of active preservation, having been acquired by new owners following use as a driver trainer in the Carlisle area. Of the other withdrawn PD3s, 16 was

Left: In early 1980 two of the 1961 PD3/4s, Nos. 17/9, were modified for use as permanent driver tuition vehicles. This view shows PRN909 (formerly No. 17) on the Moor in June 1987. As part of the work carried out the upstairs seats were removed and the top deck was isolated.

Below left: Q644GFV started out as MCW bodied Leyland PD3/4 No. 16 (PRN908) and was rebuilt for use as a recovery vehicle in 1978 being used as such until 1994. Here it is seen parked on the Ribble side of the Bus Station in February 1989.

delivered in two batches of five only a couple of weeks apart, and all entered service over the space of just seven days, towards the end of March. One prominent identifying feature of this second batch of Alexanders was the lower position of the front destination screens which made it much easier to change the blind than on the higher positioned screens fitted to Nos. 101-10. Number 141 was loaned to Lothian Regional Transport for a couple of weeks at the end of April 1981, on behalf of Leyland Vehicles, for use as a demonstrator which featured two-door bodywork on a 33ft long chassis, whilst Nos. 143/7/8 were the only members of the second batch to be rebuilt at the front, again following accidents in 8/88, 9/94 and 10/91 respectively. In the first three months of 1980 an equal number of PD3s was withdrawn, leaving just Nos. 69 and 70 to soldier on alone into 1981. In January and February respectively PD3s Nos. 19 and 17 were taken out of service and converted to permanent driver tuition vehicles which, in the event, replaced the two Leyland bodied PD2/10s, registered FRN737/8. Whilst Nos. 15, 71, 85 and 90 again all succumbed to CoF expiry, 13/4 and 72/3 continued in service until Friday 21st March, ending their days as the only four PD3s to be withdrawn as 'runners'. Later the same year the first Panthers were withdrawn beginning with Nos. 201/2 in September and continuing with 205/10/1/5 in October. The former lay derelict in the garage yard for several months and were heavily cannibalised before eventually being sold for scrap in June 1981.

taken into the Department's workshops where it underwent extensive change to finally emerge in a somewhat cut-down form for use as a purpose-built recovery vehicle which replaced ex-bus No. 6 (BCK939). The main lifting gear, which had come originally from an ex-War Department Canadian recovery vehicle, was transferred from No. 6 to the new recovery vehicle. This in turn was replaced by a brand new Seddon Atkinson purpose built Strato 400 series recovery vehicle in 1993.

Another ten Atlanteans were received in 1980 but rather surprisingly Preston reverted to Alexander for the bodywork construction. The choice of body builder may have been connected with the fact that Alexander had actually won the tender to body the second batch of chassis but at that time had been heavily committed and the order had consequently been awarded to East Lancashire. Numbers 141-50 (UHG141-50V) were similar in appearance to the first ten Alexanders but unlike their East Lancashire counterparts they were

In March 1980 a second batch of ten Alexander bodied Atlanteans entered service which replaced all but two of the remaining PD3s. Numerically first of the batch, No. 141, is seen in New Hall Lane in August 1983. This batch had lower destination boxes compared with Nos. 101-10 and as a result they were more popular with the drivers.

Seen in miserable conditions on its very last day in service, 1st November 1981, is Preston's last Titan, MCW bodied PD3A/1 No. 70 specially posed for the camera at the Longsands Lane terminus which was at the other end of the lane from the Continuation Hospital, on which working No. 70 was being employed at the time. Earlier that day it had taken part in a commemorative run for the benefit of enthusiasts.

Seven more East Lancs bodied Atlanteans entered service in April 1981 and these were the first for the Undertaking with the more rounded corners at the front. No. 152 is seen in Watling Street Road on the lightly used service from Moor Nook to Royal Preston Hospital.

Left: For many years the Ashton Lane Ends was the author's local bus route during which time it progressed from the PD1 era through to 'one-man operation' with Panthers and Atlanteans. New in February 1975 Alexander-bodied Atlantean No. 109 is seen at the terminus in Kimberley Road, in November 1980, only a matter of days before the route disappeared from the route map following a comprehensive re-organisation of services

Below left: Number 164 was twice used as a mobile information centre in connection with W.R.Tuson College (now Preston College). The 1981 East Lancs bodied Atlantean is seen in this guise for the first time, posed on the Market Square in September 1987. Its second such venture took place in June 1989.

With regard to route developments the 'eighties was a notable decade. The date 3rd November 1980 was one of the landmarks in the history of route development in Preston. From that date all services were given numbers as opposed to letters, and several service alterations took place at the same time. The Lane Ends Ashton C destination disappeared from the route map altogether, being replaced by services 33 and 44 which continued on to Tanterton and Ingol respectively. Other than certain peak hour journeys service 26 to Lea was rerouted via Garstang Road. The numbers allocated to each route corresponded with one of the Bus Station gate numbers used by each particular service with the exception of the 43/44 which doubled up with the 33/34. Appendix C gives further details of service renumberings at this time.

The Leyland Titan era came to an end when PD3A No. 69 was taken out of service at the end of July '81 and sister vehicle No. 70 was retired a couple of months later. The last day was 1st November when No. 70 was hired by the author for a commemorative run which culminated with a rostered trip on the afternoon

Continuation Hospital service. Throughout 1981 as many as fifteen Panthers were taken out of service comprising Nos. 203/4/6-9/12-4/6-9/21/2 and by the end of the year the operational fleet had fallen to 88 compared with 96 just two years earlier, and further retraction was to follow. Many of the withdrawn Panthers were stored for several months and this gave rise to space problems at the garage. Consequently, from the end of October 1980 through to mid-1981, as many as nine Panthers were variously stored in a warehouse on the docks, together with PD3 training bus PRN911 and Leyland Tiger CRN79.

Between 1981 and 1983 the final Atlanteans, all with East Lancashire bodywork, were taken into stock in four separate batches comprising :- Nos. 151-7 (GFV151-7W), 158-65 (OBV158-65X), 166-72 (URN166-72Y) and finally 173-7, 1 and 2 (DRN173-7, 1,2Y). These all had the more attractive rounded corners to the front lower body side panels and apart from Nos. 1 and 2 each batch was identical in external appearance. The latter were originally to have been 178/9 but some time before bodywork construction commenced the specification was changed and they eventually emerged as 74 coach-seated examples, featuring just a single doorway and several other detailed differences in bodywork design. They also introduced a smart new livery to the double-deck fleet which basically consisted of overall ivory with just the standard blue skirt. Three blue bands, each of a different shade, were applied between decks around the vehicles and again angled at about 20º to the vertical on each side towards the rear. Although side destination boxes were initially fitted to Nos. 1 and 2 these were soon removed and no subsequent new buses have been so equipped. Initially, for several

months after delivery, these two Atlanteans spent most of their time on service 28 (formerly the P2), which was deemed to be a quiet service and one that was less vulnerable to mindless acts of vandalism. Service 29 (Frenchwood) was also an early preserve of the coach-seated deckers when they were not required for other duties.

Returning to the main body of deliveries two Atlanteans, Nos. 153/72, were received in different base colours ready for the application of all-over advert designs. Number 153 was delivered in all-over white and 172 was likewise allover red. These were just two out of an eventual eleven advert designs carried by nine different East Lancs-bodied Atlanteans between September 1979 and October 1993. No. 164 was twice selected for temporary conversion into a mobile exhibition unit to promote work training. In September 1987 it was converted to H25/13D configuration and in June 1989 it became H13/17D, each time being additionally fitted out with tables and information screens. Both conversions were very short lived and after each occasion it reverted to its original seating layout for normal bus work. The addition of the last 29 Atlanteans to stock, together with a lone Olympian which was purchased in 1984, totally eclipsed all the remaining Panthers which were withdrawn as follows :- 1982, Nos. 220/3-8; 1983, Nos. 229-32/4/7-41 and finally in 1984, Nos. 33/5/6, with the latter having by then had their fleet numbers reduced by 200. For a few years after bus deregulation a number of former Preston Panthers could be seen working in the centre of Manchester with as many as a dozen having been acquired at least third-hand by Citibus of Middleton. However this operator later concentrated more services on double-deck vehicles and the Panthers had all moved

away by the end of 1992.

The long process of converting routes to PAYB was completed on 22nd March 1982 when service 16 (Farringdon Park) finally succumbed with the last few conductors mainly opting for early retirement. In October of that year an experimental service using one midibus and known as the Inner Link started a three month trial period operating on Saturdays only. Numbered 13, the route performed a one-way loop in a clockwise direction from the Bus Station around the periphery of the Town Centre. This service was not a success and was withdrawn at the end of the trial period. In June 1983 the long established Fulwood circular routes, the 15 and 20, were extended and altered to run out and back to/from the bus turning circle in Sharoe Green Lane. Further extensions were later made to both routes, first to Sherwood and then to Fulwood Asda. At the same time a new service, numbered 37, was introduced running to Fulwood Row routed via Garstang Road and the full length of Watling Street Road. Twelve months later services 24 (Pedders Lane Ashton) and 26 (Lea via Garstang Road) were both withdrawn and replaced by new service 25 which

Below left: East Lancs-bodied Atlantean No. 177 was only a few weeks old when photographed in July 1983 in New Hall Lane working back to town from Farringdon Park.

standardisation of the livery detail; some ten years later it was further renumbered to 133. Number 33 was to be the only Preston Olympian powered by a Leyland engine with subsequent batches receiving Cummins units.

The Ultimate ticket machine had held sway for nearly four decades but the initial threat to this hard-wearing reliable machine came in April 1984 when Atlantean 158 was fitted with a computerised ticket machine, marketed by Control Systems Ltd of Uxbridge. This was followed by similar conversions to Nos. 151-7 over a period of several months and then a further batch in January 1986, by which time all of Nos. 151-70/2 had been so treated. However, in August of that year, it was decided to adopt a more advanced model also supplied by the same company for use on the whole fleet. Atlantean 168 was the first recipient and conversion was swift with all buses having been so equipped by February of the following year; thus the Ultimate ticket machine finally bowed out in 1987. The advantages of the new machines were manifold with vast amounts of data accumulated on a daily basis which could then be transferred into the computer for storage thereby giving the Department all manner of information regarding passenger journeys and loadings etc. In July 1984 fleet number transfers were changed from the cream sans serif to the smaller NBC style silver transfers and these have been in use since on all standard size vehicles.

The two years prior to deregulation were the quietest

followed the same route as the former to Pedders Lane and then continued as the latter to Lea.

As briefly referred to previously a Leyland Olympian was purchased in February 1984. Fitted with an Eastern Coach Works 10.20m H47/27F body this vehicle had coach type seats when new and was initially allotted the fleet number 3, being registered A33MRN. The livery worn was the same as that applied to Atlanteans 1 and 2 although the multi-coloured blue bands were slightly thinner. On the in-between decks panels, on each side, was the lettering *'Leyland Bus Olympian Demonstrator'* and it was used as such by Leyland Vehicles between May 1984 and July 1985 during which time it visited many towns and cities throughout the mainland. Originally it did not carry its allotted fleet number 3 and was renumbered to 33 in February 1985 at which time it was given a full repaint with the removal of the demonstration lettering and

Right: Numbers 1 and 2 were the last two of the final batch of seven Atlanteans received from East Lancs in June 1983. As is clearly illustrated in this view of the duo, taken at the garage just before their first engagement, their specification and livery arrangement differed somewhat from the remainder of the batch.

Below right: Number 33 was an ECW bodied Leyland Olympian which came to Preston in February 1984. However, for the first fifteen months it was used as a demonstrator by Leyland Vehicles during which time it visited many towns and cities throughout the mainland. Here No. 33 is caught by the camera in Tag Lane, Ingol, in September 1985; it eventually received standard bus livery and lost its DP seats during an internal refit in October '93.

period in the history of Preston's municipal buses. No new buses were purchased in 1985 and 1986 and no withdrawals took place either. At the end of 1984 the fleet size had dipped to an all-time post-war low of 83 and with the future then looking somewhat uncertain due to the advent of bus deregulation, Preston Transport, in line with many other bus companies, was content to await developments before committing itself to a future bus replacement programme. However, a short time before the implementation of deregulation, in August 1986, four second-hand 11.3m

long Leyland Nationals joined the fleet. These were registered YFY1,2,7,8M and were given fleet numbers 5-8. Originally dual-doored buses purchased new by Southport Corporation in 1974 they passed with that undertaking to Merseyside PTE later the same year and were rebuilt to single door format in 9/80 (5 and 6), 10/80 (7) and 4/81 (8). They were acquired in full Merseyside livery of jonquil green and cream with a brown skirt and entered service so painted with the addition of '*Borough of Preston*' fleetnames. The intention was to use them only on school contract work, the first tenders for which were to commence in September 1986. Full destination blinds were later fitted and they did see occasional use on ordinary stage services, particularly service 25 to Lea. Number 6 (YFY2M) was withdrawn prematurely in July 1987, as the result of an accident, but the others continued in service until November 1989 by which time they had become surplus to requirements. Rather

strangely they remained in '*as acquired*' livery until 1/88 (7) and 8/88 (5 and 8) when they were eventually treated to a full repaint in Preston colours of blue and ivory also receiving '*Preston Bus*' fleetnames. Whilst No. 6 was sold to Burnley & Pendle Transport for use as a source of spares the other three returned to Merseyside, following their purchase in February 1990 by North Western for whom they were still running at the time of writing in 1995. From 18th August 1986 a network of free services started running from various outlying districts to a new ASDA store situated in Fulwood with buses being provided by Preston Transport using a maximum of three Atlanteans. From 3rd December 1990 the services passed to Ribble which continued to provide a similar level of service.

5. POST DEREGULATION

(From October 1986)

The last months of 1986 and the early part of 1987 could have been described as the calm before the storm. The 26th October 1986 was a very important date for Preston, just as it was for every other operator in the country. The newly formed *Preston Borough Transport Ltd.* immediately effected several service changes, the most significant of which involved service 30 to Savick which was rerouted to a new terminus in Savick Way and at the same time converted back to standard bus operation. This, together with the withdrawal of service 12 to Grange, spelt the end for the Bristol LHS midibuses and consequently Nos. 42-4 were withdrawn en bloc in January 1987, with all three passing to Busways Travel Services Ltd of Newcastle. Number 42 was noted still in existence in 1994 on the island of Jersey, painted red and re-registered with a Jersey mark. Deregulation also saw the end of joint Preston/Ribble operations and service 43, which had latterly been the only service thus operated, became solely run by Preston vehicles. Deregulation day didn't bring any new competition and after the initial flourish of service changes six months of relative calm followed; but all this was soon to change with the announcement that United Transport Buses Ltd. were to start operations in Preston with a fleet of minibuses. Preston had always welcomed fair competition and had operated amicably for many years alongside the likes of Ribble, Fishwick, Scout, Bamber Bridge Motor Services, Viking and Mercers, to name but a few. However the twelve months from

Above: In August 1986 Preston acquired four Leyland Nationals from MPTE specifically for school contract work and which initially retained the PTE livery of jonquil green & cream. They did occasionally see use on stage services as illustrated here by No. 6 which has been caught alongside Ashton Park in Blackpool Road working through to Lea. Only a few weeks later it was unfortunately written off in an accident

Left: Seen on the Moor in March 1989 are Nos. 7 and 8, two further examples of the Leyland Nationals acquired from Merseyside PTE. Here the pair look very smart in Preston livery which was only applied the previous year.

Right: The three Bristol LHS midibuses carried three sets of fleet numbers whilst in use with Preston. With its second number, No. 344 departs the Bus Station in June 1983 bound for Savick Estate. All three were sold to Busways of Newcastle in January 1987.

Below: Number 67 was one of three Northern Counties Dodge minibuses that were received with 20 DP type seats (Nos. 70/1 being the other two), although this particular bus was later reseated with ordinary bus seats. This view was taken at the 19 terminus in the Royal Preston Hospital grounds in June 1987.

April 1987 were to prove a testing time for the new Undertaking as United Transport gradually introduced a full network of Preston town services, marketed as 'Zippy', which penetrated into all the outlying districts of the town and beyond. The bright yellow and red buses were mainly Ivecos or Freight Rover Sherpas, although ten Talbot Pullman three-axle buses were also operated within a maximum fleet size of 75 vehicles.

Preston Bus lost no time in responding and placed an order for 20 Northern Counties-bodied Dodge minibuses which comprised 18 of the 'S56' model and two of the narrower 'S46' type. The Dodge chassis was powered by a Perkins engine and those taken by Preston entered the fleet as Nos. 50-69 (D750-69YCW). When new all but one had seating for 22; the exception being No. 67 which was fitted with 20 high-backed seats. However this vehicle was reseated in January 1994 to B20F, after exchanging seats with a similar former Merseyside PTE. example. Reflecting the haste with which the Dodges had been ordered the seats were 'off the shelf' covered in a dark red moquette instead of the in-house turquoise blue with red, white and black stripes. Attractive '*Preston Mini*' fleetnames were applied to the sides and back and the fleet number decals were the black style applied to Greater Manchester buses; no doubt so as not to delay delivery any longer than absolutely necessary. Numbers 68/9 were the 'S46' models and had manual gearboxes to enable them to be used as driver training vehicles. The first of these

entered service on 21st April at exactly the same time as the first Zippy minibuses and were introduced to existing services 27 and 30, running to Larches and Savick Estates respectively. At the same time a completely new service, numbered 19, commenced running to the Royal Preston Hospital via Deepdale Road, Watling Street Road and Sharoe Green Lane. It also used private roads inside the hospital grounds and this proved to be a major factor in its success since later in the battle for passengers Zippy were unable to gain the same advantage. The three minibus services started on a low basic frequency since from the outset there were not sufficient buses available to provide high frequency services. Initially minibus service 27 operated as an addition to the existing 27 with each service having its own unco-ordinated timetable. Minibus service 30 was a somewhat different route from the one it had replaced. The new route followed the same roads as the 27 as far as Fylde Road from where it then continued to run via Tulketh Road, Egerton Road, Pedders Lane, Cottam Lane and

Two of the first twenty Dodge minibuses received in April 1987 were the narrower 'S46' type with manual gears numbered 68/9. In this view No. 69 is seen at the Larches Estate terminus when only in its second month of service.

D40AFV, a Duple bodied Leyland Tiger, was received in April 1987 for Private Hire and Excursion work. In this view taken in September 1991 No. 40 has been captured setting out from the Bus Station on a day excursion. In December 1994 it was reregistered to PRN909 taking the mark from a former Preston PD3 and shortly afterwards it was renumbered to 309.

West Park Avenue to Savick. By 1st June service 19 was operating every five minutes during the day, on Mon-Sat, whilst at the same time services 27 and 30 each provided a fifteen minute frequency. A fourth minibus service started on 11th May, numbered 114, which ran via the 14 route to Holme Slack and then continued along Ronaldsway to Lambert Road and Fairfax Road.

Prior to receiving any of its own minibuses Preston had taken three on loan from other concerns for assessment and driver familiarisation. These were D912NBA, a Northern Counties demonstrator and two Freight Rover Sherpas, registered D861/2LWR, from Yorkshire Rider of Leeds. Two more 'S56' models were delivered in May as Nos. 70/1 (D870/1ABV) and these were also fitted with 20 high backed seats. Also at this time Preston took delivery of its first and so far only luxury coach, No. 40 (D40AFV). This was a Leyland Tiger with a 51-seat 11.3m Duple 320 (3.2m high) body and was bought for the specific purpose of Private Hire

and Excursion work of which it has subsequently seen plenty of use. The livery worn by No. 40 amounted to a single-deck version of the three blue band arrangement worn by Nos. 1, 2 and 33 with *'Preston Coach'* fleetnames. Before the year was out more Dodge/ Northern Counties minibuses were added to the fleet in the shape of Nos. 41-3 (D41-3AFV), 44 (E44FFV), 45/ 6 (E45/6GRN), and 72-4 (D72-4AFV). It was only in June '87 that the *'Borough of Preston'* fleetname began to be replaced by the new *'Preston Bus'* insignia. Besides being applied to the sides of the vehicles it was also positioned on the front, above the destination screen, accompanied by one of four slogans which read either *'Your Friendly Service'*, *'We Care'*, *'For Easy Shopping'* or lastly, *'The Best Bus in Town'*. Eventually all the Atlanteans were so adorned except the Alexander-bodied examples, 101-10. Numbers 102-7 were withdrawn in September and passed to the North Western Road Car Co Ltd with 103 being substituted for 108 at

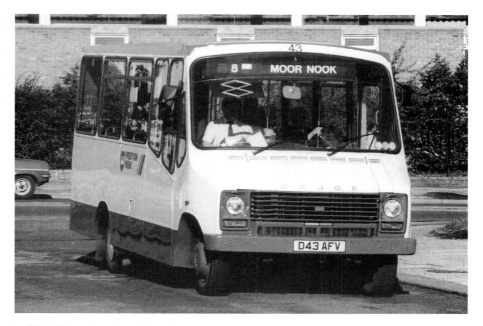

Number 43 was one of 31 Dodge minibuses with this B22F style of Northern Counties bodywork which entered service with Preston in 1987. This view was taken in Ribbleton Hall Lane in September 1987 working one of the many minibus services which were introduced at that time.

1980-built Alexander bodied Atlantean No. 149 is pictured in Blackpool Road in February 1989 nearing its journey's end. Note the 'Best Bus' slogan on the front, one of four different linguistic annotations which were similarly applied to virtually all the Atlantean fleet in 1987

the last minute, at the request of North Western, to make up a numerical run. They were quickly repainted into North Western's striking red, blue and grey livery and given fleet numbers 492-7. Initially allocated to that operator's Altrincham garage they could be found in the late 'eighties working into Manchester where they then rubbed shoulders with other former Preston buses in the form of Citibus's Panthers. By 1994 they had gravitated to Merseyside and were working out of Bootle garage.

Meanwhile the battle with Zippy for customers continued unabated. The 13th July had brought another round of service changes. Services 5 and 6 to Brookfield (and Longsands Lane) were completely withdrawn whilst the remaining service to Brookfield, the 7, was a further conversion to minibus operation. Similarly, service 8 to Moor Nook was also converted to minibus operation and at the same time it was substantially rerouted to circle the Moor Nook estate. Meanwhile minibus service 114 replaced the parallel service 14 in the evenings and

on Sundays. The Broadgate service also gained minibuses on this latter day. Alterations were not only confined to minibus routes with several major revisions also affecting standard bus routes. Service 10 to Ribbleton Gamull Lane was withdrawn with all departures to Ribbleton forthwith operating as service 11 via Grange Estate. In Fulwood services 15 and 20 to Sherwood/ASDA were withdrawn with the latter part of the route being covered by new service 23, which operated during the day alternately with service 22, running by way of the same route as the latter to Sharoe Green Lane and then continuing via Sherwood Way and Eastway to Sherwood/ASDA. In the evenings and on Sundays the 22 was withdrawn in favour of the longer route 23. At the times buses only operated as far as Sherwood the route number 123 was generally displayed. The Ingol area routes also saw several changes with the 34 and 44 being re-routed to serve Redcar Avenue and Whitby Avenue and in addition the 33 from Tanterton was re-routed, inward

This August 1981 view depicts 1976 East Lancs bodied Atlantean No. 112 at the Longsands Lane terminus. This very infrequent service, which was a projection of certain Fulwood Row journeys, was discontinued after July 1987. After returning to the Bus Station No. 112 will then work through to Broadgate .

only, via Plungington Road and Adelphi Street vice Brook Street. The object of this latter exercise was to put more buses onto Plungington Road, running into town, to combat the introduction of Zippy's Z4 and Z14 routes which had been introduced to serve various parts of Fulwood and operated mainly in direct competition with Preston routes 22 and 23.

There was to be no let up in the battle with United Transport and service revisions continued apace with

the introduction of new Zippy routes. From 17th August new minibus service 24 to Fulwood, Conway Drive, commenced operation running off-peak on Mon-Fri only. This service was worked exclusively by Dodge 44 which was fitted with extra luggage space and originally had two fewer seats than the rest of the type, being B20F from new. Unfortunately the 24 was started at the same time as a more frequent parallel Zippy route and consequently it was not a success, being withdrawn after

The penultimate batch of East Lancs bodied Atlanteans was received in late 1982. Here No. 169 was less than a year old when pictured in Miller Road in August 1983. The Moor Nook service was one of the many services which were converted to minibus operation in the late 1980s.

Alexander-bodied Atlantean No. 143 was one of three of the batch which were modified at the front following minor collision damage; the others being Nos. 147/8. This view shows No. 143 departing the Bus Station in March 1989 on the short lived service to Broughton and Woodplumpton.

only eight weeks of operation. When Preston had withdrawn service 6 the Deepdale Road corridor to Brookfield was left to Zippy, whilst the former was content to serve the area solely with the frequent service 19. However, Zippy altered the routing of its Brookfield service and Preston duly stepped in to fill the gap with the reintroduction of service 6 on 12th October but now using minibuses and rerouted around various minor roads on the estate. November also saw the introduction of a new out of town service which operated to Broughton and Woodplumpton using standard size buses. Numbered 31, six return journeys were provided off-peak on Mon-Fri and the service was routed to run via the A6 to Broughton cross-roads and then describe a large anti-clockwise circle through Woodplumpton and Tanterton and back to the A6 at its junction with Lightfoot Lane.

The following year, 1988, saw a continuation of the trend set the previous year. Another 19 Dodge/Renault minibuses were taken into stock, again fitted with Northern Counties bodywork but with a slightly longer (6.9m) 25-seat restyled version. These comprised Nos. 47 (E47KBV), 48/9 (E48/9MCK), 75-7 (E75-7LFR), 78-87 (E78-87MHG) and 88-90 (F88-90UHG) with all but the last three having been received by May. It had not originally been envisaged how many minibuses would eventually enter the fleet and the resultant number sequence became somewhat erratic. Having first started at No. 50 it was decided, for some unknown reason, to jump back to 41 starting with the June '87 deliveries. Eventually the block up to 49 was filled with these nine numbers actually comprising five separate batches. With regard to Nos. 75-7, these were delivered with fleet and registration numbers which did not tally with the chassis and body numbers recorded on the ownership forms, and consequently the three buses swapped identities in November 1988 when 75 became 77, 76

In February 1988 the first of the B25F restyled Northern Counties bodied Renault/Dodges entered the fleet in the shape of Nos. 47, 75-7. No. 75 is seen passing the Town Hall in Lancaster Road on a Sunday morning trip to Penwortham in June of that year.

Number 49 was another Renault/Dodge with the later style of B25F Northern Counties bodywork and was new in March 1988. It is seen here in Friargate returning from Penwortham on service 4 which was one of three out of town minibus services introduced in competition with the Ribble 'Zippy' operations. Only Nos. 47-9,75-7 originally had the outline Preston name on the front.

Number 78 was the first of a further ten 25 seat Northern Counties Renault/Dodge minibuses, which were hastily received in April 1988. This view shows No. 78 on the Sunday working of the short lived service 39 to Blackpool and is taken in Blackpool Road, Ashton, in July 1988. On M-S the 39 was worked by Atlanteans.

became 75 and finally 77 became 76. These three, along with Nos. 47-9, initially carried large '**_PRESTON_**' names in blue outline letters on the front which were similar in style to those applied by Chester City Transport to their own Dodges. In July '94 No. 77 was the subject of an internal revamp when, amongst other modifications, the seats were recovered in the standard blue moquette and the soft trim on the internal lower body sides was removed.

From 1st February 1988 standard buses returned to the Larches route mainly as service 127 journeys, which either continued to or started from Lea. Various other minibus services continued to see a few scheduled standard bus operated journeys with the principal exceptions being the 19 and 114. The 11th April brought another round of service changes with several routes gaining enhanced frequencies and a further increase in minibus operation. Service 5 to Brookfield was reinstated using minibuses, thereby completing the reinstatement

of this group of routes. The Broadgate (21) and Ingol Redcar Avenue (43) also gained minibuses, although the latter was basically a completely different route whilst the opportunity was also taken to reroute the Broadgate via more residential roads. One strange quirk which resulted from the need to balance the various minibus workings was the use of them for alternate journeys to Frenchwood (service 29). Preston now operated minibus services to Brookfield (service Nos. 5, 6, 7), Moor Nook (8), Royal Preston Hospital (19), Broadgate (21), Larches Estate (27), Frenchwood (29), Savick (30), Ingol (43) and Holme Slack (114). However, after only one year of operation United Transport sold the Zippy operations to Ribble, which acquired all the vehicles and continued to operate the Zippy network of services. So the main threat of competition came from Ribble and Preston turned its attention towards that operator. These were interesting and testing times for the new undertaking.

Two more of the many Dodge/Renault minibuses which entered the fleet in 1987/8 are seen together at the Bus Station in March 1989. Nos. 80 and 89 were of separate batches but both carried the B25F style of Northern Counties bodywork.

At the same time as the minibus explosion was taking place a solitary 85 seat Northern Counties bodied Olympian entered the fleet as No. 32. Originally the route number and destination screens were on opposite sides but following complaints from the drivers they were altered to the normal format, as this view taken in Tag Lane in September 1991 testifies. It was renumbered to 132 in February

Besides running on Preston town services Zippy had also operated a number of minibus services to outlying areas such as Penwortham, Longton, Lostock Hall and Bamber Bridge, all of which had initially competed with Ribble and Fishwick. In retaliation for Ribble keeping the local Zippy routes running Preston introduced two more daily minibus services on 16th May, running out-of-town to nearby Penwortham and Bamber Bridge, numbered 4 and 17 (with associated infrequent 126 service) respectively. Twelve months later a third out of town minibus service was started, numbered 3, which operated to Longton. On the three aforementioned services the driver gave change, unlike all of Preston's other services, since they were competing with other operators' services which also provided this facility. Preston also tried its hand at inter-town working with the introduction, on 16th July, of service 39 which operated daily to Blackpool Talbot Road Bus Station and incorporated a section of motorway running via the

M55 between Wesham and the outskirts of Blackpool. The 39 departed from the Ribble side of the Bus Station (shades of the Ingol P4) and in effect it actually ran in conjunction with Lancaster City Transport's service 41 and employed standard buses on Mon-Sat and minibuses on Sundays. The 39 last operated on 18th November 1988 and was not reinstated for the 1989 summer season. One further new service to Lea, which was introduced on the 5th December, used the number 24 for the third time. Again operation was with minibuses running as service 25 but additionally serving Thorntrees Avenue and Hawthorn Crescent. By the end of 1988 a total of 50 minibuses had been amassed out of a grand fleet total of 128. The introduction of all these new buses caused space problems at the garage and a number of minibuses were packed tight into the workshop space overnight and on Sundays. To some extent this is still the case although a secure compound has been built in the garage yard to hold in the region of twelve minibuses.

In March 1989 Preston took delivery of its first new single-deckers for some considerable time in the form of four Leyland Lynxes. No. 10 is seen when brand new descending Friargate on the Sunday variant of service 23 to Sherwood. Nos. 10/1 of an eventual 15 Lynxes were the only two with ordinary bus seats with all the rest having the DP type.

Two further Northern Counties/Dodges were added to the fleet in April 1989 as Nos. 91/2 (F91/2AHG). The previous month had seen the introduction of Preston's first new double-decker for five years in the form of Leyland Olympian No. 32 (F32AHG). The complete vehicle had a 10.4m long Northern Counties body with seating for 85 passengers in the configuration of H51/34F. Following the trend set towards single-doored buses by Atlanteans 1 and 2 this was maintained on all subsequent additions to the fleet. Side destination boxes were no longer specified, although use was still made of them on vehicles so fitted. No. 32's destination and route number blinds were deliberately transposed in position, as a recommendation of DiPTAC (**Di**sabled **P**ersons **T**ransport **A**dvisory **C**ommittee), but this proved to be hugely unpopular with the drivers and the layout was eventually altered to conform with the rest of the fleet. As part of a rationalised numbering scheme implemented in early 1995, 32 later became 132. March 1989 also saw a return to new single-deck buses with the purchase of four Leyland Lynx with Cummins L10 engines, as Nos. 10-13 (F210-13YHG). The first two were fitted out with 47 bus type seats whilst the latter two had 45 coach type

In November 1989 five more Leyland Lynxes were put into service. First of the batch, No. 14, is seen in New Hall Lane in September 1991 on the frequent Farringdon Park service.

This February 1981 view depicts Marshall Camair bodied Leyland Panther No. 240 in Ashworth Grove, Frenchwood, alongside the north bank of the river Ribble. One of the first bus services, the Frenchwood service ceased to run in October 1989 and the district is now served by Stagecoach Ribble.

seats. A feature of these Workington built models was the deep side windows with bonded glazing, a form of construction which the bodyshop personnel had to quickly become familiar with in order to perform the relatively routine task of replacing damaged windows. Other significant features of the Lynx were the squared off wheel arches and the angled back flat windscreen in front of the driver. Before the end of the year a further five Lynxes, Nos. 14-18 (G214-18KRN), all with coach type seats, were added to stock. The ten new buses replaced an equal number of existing standard size buses which comprised the last of the GBV/N Alexander-bodied Atlanteans, 101/8-10; three of the UFV/R East Lancs batch, 113/5/8, and the remaining three Leyland Nationals. Whilst the Atlanteans initially went into store, pending disposal, the Nationals gravitated back to Merseyside and ended up with North Western Road Car working out of Bootle garage alongside former Preston Atlanteans.

Eventually the level of post deregulation activity subsided and the pattern of services operated remained unaltered until 16th October 1989, when another round of service changes took place. At this time Preston ceased to operate on out-of-town services and Ribble reduced its in-town activity to more or less the pre-Zippy level of operations. Consequently services 3, 4 ,17 and 31 were all withdrawn entirely but at the same time several more new services were introduced to fill the

gaps left by the withdrawal of Ribble 'Zippy' operations. New minibus services which commenced at this time ran to Moor Nook via New Hall Lane and to Savick via Brook Street which were given the route numbers 9 and 31 respectively. Both these services were direct replacements for former Zippy routes. In conjunction with the conversion of Ingol services 34 and 44 to minibus a new service using standard buses commenced operation to Tanterton, numbered 35, which was routed via Fylde Road and Tulketh Brow. To complete the alterations, one of the original three bus routes, the Frenchwood service (29), was withdrawn with the district being left for Ribble to serve, which was quite appropriate since Ribble's Head Office and Preston Depot were both situated in the area. These were followed by additional route alterations to services 10, 23 and 114 in January 1990.

Whilst all the Atlanteans had been delivered as two-door 82-seaters (except Nos. 1 and 2), in February 1990 it was decided to evaluate the conversion of one Atlantean to single-door format, with a resultant increase in seating capacity due to the removal of the centre exit. Number 154 was chosen and following its rebuilding its seating capacity was increased by four, thus making it H50/36F. At the same time many DiPTAC features were added, which included the insertion of an intermediate step at the entrance, the addition of more grab rails painted in a more distinctive colour to aid the

Originally all except the last two Atlanteans had dual door bodywork. However, following a pilot scheme to rebuild No. 154 to single doorway in February 1990, it was decided to similarly convert all of Nos. 141-77. One of the last to be treated in November 1992 was East Lancs No. 155 which is seen outside the garage a few weeks later.

visually handicapped, and the addition of more bell pushes in more accessible positions. It was decided that the conversion of the Atlantean fleet to single-door was a worthwhile and viable proposition and consequently all of Nos. 141-77 were progressively rebuilt with the last, No. 152, being completed in June 1993. The Alexander bodied batch, Nos. 141-50, only gained three extra seats thus becoming H49/36F. Although all the

Atlanteans eventually received DiPTAC features the work was not necessarily carried out at the same time as the door conversions.

Following the trend back to conventional buses in 1989 an even more welcome reversal was the purchase of four new double-deckers in March 1990. These were Leyland-bodied Olympians 34-7 (G34-7OCK) which were fitted out with 72 coach seats (34/5) and 78 bus

This scene at the Bus Station was taken in July 1990 and depicts 1979 East Lancs bodied Atlantean No. 133 alongside the virtually then brand new Leyland Olympian No. 36. The latter was one of a batch of four received in March of that year but only Nos. 36/7 had bus type seats with the other two, Nos. 34/5, having DP seating.

No. 34 was one of the two dual purpose seated Leyland bodied Olympians which entered service in March 1990. In this view it is seen in Sedgwick Street later that year on the relatively short Holme Slack service. Nos. 34-7 became 134-7 in early 1995.

seats (36/7) respectively. Curiously they also had side and rear route number boxes, which were apparently another DiPTAC recommendation, but to date they have never been used. Although the complete vehicles were built by Leyland at the Workington factory the body style was very similar to the ECW design, since Leyland had transferred production from Lowestoft in 1987 following the closure of ECW. Number 34 is the only one of the quartet which has not subsequently carried an all-over advert colour scheme. Along with Nos. 32/3 they were renumbered into the 1xx series in early 1995. These replaced further East Lancs-bodied Atlanteans, on a one-to-one basis, in the form of Nos. 116/7/9/20. Before the end of the year all of this latter batch were to have been withdrawn.

At the beginning of October eleven withdrawn Atlanteans were still in store at the garage comprising Nos. 101/8-10/3/5-20. That month 101 went on loan to Hyndburn Transport which showed an interest in purchasing some of the withdrawn stock and indeed did eventually take the four Alexander-bodied examples, 101/8-10. However, as part of the conditions of purchase, Hyndburn requested that the centre doors be removed by Preston. Number 108 was the first to be dealt with in November, followed by 109 in December. The former was also painted into Hyndburn livery in the Deepdale paintshop. Due to the fact that a programme of door conversions was already underway on the Department's own Atlanteans, Preston did not have the capacity at the time to complete all the work for Hyndburn and consequently the work on Nos. 101/10 was sub-contracted out to a firm trading as S. & T., situated at Intack in Blackburn. Final painting on all four was carried out at Preston with 110 the last to be finished in March '91, although 109 was actually painted in all-over white as the base colour for an advert which was again completed by an outside contractor.

In November, after an absence of more than two years, the all-over advert returned to the Preston fleet

when Atlantean 177 and Renault minibus 83 were both painted thus for different sponsors. One significant difference from previous applications was the retention of fleet livery on the fronts of the vehicles, deemed advantageous in what was now a much more competitive bus world. Incidentally it was the second time that 177 had been selected for an all-over 'Ad' and it wasn't to be the last either. At the same time as all this was going on, four of the withdrawn East Lancs batch passed to Warrington Borough Transport in the form of Nos. 113/6/7/20, but again Warrington requested that the centre doors be removed before the sale was completed. These were again dealt with by S. & T. but this time the repainting was carried out by the purchaser. By the year-end only 115/8/9 remained of the long-term withdrawn stock, but these had now been joined by further displaced Atlanteans in the form of 111/2/4, the last of the UFV/R batch and 121-5 of the 1977 East Lancs batch. With the withdrawal of 124/5 in December the fleet size actually dipped by two to 128.

In what was proving to be a very busy time for the undertaking the first four of six more Leyland Lynxes were also received that month being identical in all respects to the other high-backed seat examples already in the fleet, and these were given the numbers 23/4/6-9 with matching H/YBV registration marks. The peculiar number sequence resulted from the desire to secure matching registrations which had become more difficult to obtain since the Vehicle Licensing Authority had removed quite a lot of numbers from general issue. The last two, although received in early December, did not enter service until January '91. Number 27 almost certainly became the first Preston bus (as such) to travel overseas when in September 1992 it was used by a group of volunteer firemen to undertake an Aid Mission to Romania. For the trip No. 27 was down-seated to 25 to make room for the aid parcels and '*GB*' stickers and '*We Care*' logos were attached to the rear and sides of the vehicle respectively. It left Preston on 28th September

The final batch of six Leyland Lynxes entered service with Preston in the last two months of 1990. All had DP style seats clearly illustrated here by No. 27 seen in Tanterton Hall Road in September 1991. This was the bus which visited Romania on an aid mission in the autumn of the following year.

In January 1991 Preston acquired four second-hand Dodge minibuses to operate the newly gained Riversway Park & Ride service. No. 7, pictured at the Bus Station during a meal break in August 1991, was originally No. 32 in the Cumberland Motor Services fleet and carried a B23F Reeve Burgess body.

returning two weeks later on 12th October. All the Lynxes were renumbered into the 2xx series in early 1995.Whilst in August of that year No. 229 was the subject of an extensive rebuilding exercise in order to reduce maintenance and repair costs.

From 13th January 1991 several town centre streets were permanently closed to vehicular traffic and regrettably the ban was also extended to buses, which resulted in a reorganisation of town centre routes and bus stops. For the first time in the history of Preston's town services no public transport served the upper part of Friargate or passed the Market Square. Needless to say these alterations were not popular with the operators or the travelling public alike since intending passengers now had to wait at a recommissioned stop on Ringway, which was far more inhospitable and inconvenient than the previous stops in Harris Street and Friargate. In addition the use of Ringway, with its traffic congestion,

only served to disrupt the operators' schedules. At the end of the month the docklands area gained another route in the form of minibus service 29 whilst at the same time Preston Bus started operating the Lancashire County Council/Preston Borough Council jointly sponsored Riversway Park & Ride service which had been won on tender from Ribble. This popular amenity service was provided throughout the day, on Mon-Sat, using four acquired Dodge minibuses. Although the acquisitions were made from three different operators they actually started life with only two; D456/8/9BEO were former Barrow Borough Transport 22-seat East Lancs bodied Dodges acquired via the Stagecoach group, whilst D32SAO was also a Dodge but with a 23-seat Reeve Burgess body which came from Cumberland Motor Services. Preston gave these fleet numbers 6, 8, 9 and 7 respectively. Numbers 8 and 9 originally carried advert colour schemes, both being painted into fleet

Four shorter versions of the Northern Counties bodywork were mounted on further Olympian chassis obtained in March 1991 which were numbered 101-4. Seen at the top of Church Street, opposite the Parish Church, in September of that year, is the last of the quartet No. 104.

livery as late as 4/92 (9) and 4/94 (8); No. 6 entered service painted all white ready for the application of an advert but it never received one although later it received Park & Ride lettering on an ivory and grey livery layout, whilst No. 7 was painted in fleet livery from the outset.

In March 1991 four Olympians with Northern Counties 77-seat bodywork entered the fleet as numbers 101-4 (H101-4BFR). These were a shorter version of No. 32 but were similar in external appearance, and inside the seating split was 47 on the upper deck and 30 on the lower deck. Atlanteans 126-30 were replaced with the Olympians and these together with all the remaining undisposed Atlantean stock all went to the recently formed South Yorkshire operator, Sheffield Omnibus, based in the outlying city district of Ecclesfield. Between April and August the trend towards bus

Three of the four Dodge minibuses acquired for the Riversway Park & Ride service carried East Lancs bodywork and were originally new to Barrow B.T. in December 1986. After carrying an all white livery for the first 22 months No. 6 was painted into this promotional livery in November 1992 and is pictured at the Riversway site later the same month.

The last new double deckers received by Preston were eight Leyland Olympians which entered service in February and March 1992. No. 107, which along with No. 114 was fitted out with 72 DP type seats, had actually been assembled by October 1991 to enable it to be displayed at the biannual Coach and Bus exhibition at the NEC. This promotional Guild 1992 livery was carried from new until January 1993.

(Author's Collection)

advertising continued. Whilst Nos. 32/3 both gained full height rear-end adverts 35/7 gained all-over adverts; the former was a colourful affair advertising various events connected with Guild '92. At the beginning of August another Olympian, registered J976PRW, made the briefest of visits to the Deepdale workshops. This was a 78-seat Leyland-bodied version which would eventually become number 106, as the first of a batch of eight due for delivery early the following year. However it was first registered and used as a demonstrator by Leyland Volvo, which accounted for it having an 'RW' registration marque. In November the tender on contract service 184 to Salwick was relinquished to Redline Travel. This infrequent Mon-Sat service had been gained in July 1988 and Preston Bus had latterly operated the service with minibuses, possibly because it traversed the narrow Mill Lane, on which was also situated a bridge with a three tons weight limit.

As previously stated 1992 was another Preston Guild year, a year long celebration which only takes place once every 20 years. In February, the second of the eight Leyland-bodied Olympians arrived in the shape of No. 107 (J107KCW). This vehicle was fitted out with 72 high-backed seats in the configuration CH43/29F and was painted in a special commemorative Guild livery but still using the blue and ivory colours – and it looked very smart indeed. Number 107 had also paid a brief visit to Preston, in October '91, before going to the NEC at Birmingham, where it was displayed at the biannual Coach and Bus Exhibition. Following this it returned to the Leyland Works at Lillyhall where it remained until the rest of the batch had been constructed. These were

Nos. 108-10/2-4 (J108-10/2-4KCW) and they were delivered to Preston in March. Preston's Olympians were the last double-deck vehicles to be built at the Lillyhall, Workington, plant before the lack of orders for new buses brought about closure of the factory. All except 114 had H47/31F Leyland bodies with the former having a similar seating layout to 107. Number 106 (J976PRW) returned to Preston on 2nd April and the eight new buses effectively replaced Atlanteans 131-8, although the remaining two of the batch, 139/40, followed soon afterwards without replacement. They were initially stored for possible further use during Guild week but in the event they passed to Sheffield Omnibus en bloc before the main Guild events took place.

Over the years various demonstrators have been taken on loan for evaluation purposes but it was unusual to have two at the same time. At the beginning of September both J110SPB, a 50-seat Alexander-bodied Dennis Lance, and J363BNW, a 23-seat Optare Metrorider, were used by the undertaking. However it is unlikely that this was a complete coincidence since the first week of September was Guild week and Preston Bus needed every bus it could lay its hands on to cope with the extra demands made at this time. Generally as far as route alterations are concerned 1992 will solely be remembered for the activities during Guild week at the beginning of September. Unlike the 1972 Guild, when the Bus Station was completely closed at the times of the main processions, this time access was generally maintained, although numerous extensive diversions were required to maintain services. However, some routes were affected more than others and buses on services 21, 26, 27 and 30 were terminated at the Railway Station during the procession times. Interestingly the private station approach road was opened up to accommodate several temporary bus stands and presented a vision of what could be achieved with a better integrated transport system. At this time the Riversway Park & Ride service was complemented by six other Park & Ride services, four of which were operated by Preston Bus. Several late departures were operated to most districts at 23.30hrs and 00.10hrs on the Mon-Fri (31/8, 1/9 to 4/9), whilst on the Saturday (5/9), the day of the torchlight procession and firework display, special late night departures to all districts departed from outside Debenhams store in Fishergate at 23.45hrs, with extras being required into the small hours of Sunday morning.

On the afternoon of 3rd September there were 128 buses in use at the same time, which comprised 120 out of 129 Preston vehicles, the two demonstrators and six hired in, two of which were Hyndburn Nos. 209/10, former Preston Alexander/Atlanteans 109/10. Also worthy of note was the use of one of the hired vehicles, namely City of Lancaster open-top Atlantean UBV84L on stage services 16 and 33 besides its intended use on special work. Also in September Preston Bus took delivery of a brand new recovery vehicle in the form of K288HNG, a Seddon Atkinson Strato 400; however it was to be February 1993 before it was fully commissioned for use and even then Q644GFV remained in use alongside the Seddon for a few more months until September, when it was finally taken out of use. Atlantean 158 had spent some time in the bodyshop being fitted

out internally to full DiPTAC specification and it attended a DiPTAC convention in Blackpool on 24/5th. September. As part of its mini revamp it received '*Day-Glo*' blinds which have since become standard and are gradually being fitted in all of Preston's buses.

A new venture in 1992 was the running of regular advertised trips to Blackpool to view the illuminations. These ran every Thursday and Friday from the 17th September to 6th November and usually one of the coach-seated Atlanteans was provided. Although the venture was not repeated the following year it did reappear for the 1994 season. The only other major event of the year was the introduction of a new minibus service to Ribbleton Gamull Lane, on 10th December. Numbered 10 it was routed via the Grange Estate, an area which Preston had neglected since the cessation of service 12 in October 1986. The reason for the introduction of this route as such lay in the emergence of another competitor in the form of the Lancashire Rose Taxi Bus Co, whose services had targeted the Ribbleton Lane and New Hall Lane corridors. Although at the time Lancashire Rose had only a few vehicles, all of which were licensed as taxis with a capacity for only eight passengers, they were seen as a potential threat to certain Preston routes. In consequence Preston Bus registered, and operated, enhanced timetables on services 11 (Ribbleton Gamull Lane) and 16 (Farringdon Park) at various times to combat the operations of Lancashire Rose and later, in July '93, Savastrip tickets were made available on the 9 and 16, both of which served the New Hall Lane corridor.

Following the 1992 Guild there was somewhat of a lull in vehicle activity although both Olympians Nos. 35 and 107 lost their Guild adverts in favour of normal fleet livery early in the new year. In April 1993 the Undertaking was privatised becoming the subject of a management and employee buyout and consequently all formal links with the borough were broken although the new company, now trading as Preston Bus Ltd, continued to liaise with the council on relevant issues. In June the

New in February 1992 Leyland bodied Olympian No. 110 is pictured in October of that year in Black Bull Lane approaching Lytham Road roundabout, which was the terminus of the very first bus route inaugurated 70 years earlier, in January 1922.

last Atlantean door conversion was completed and attention was then turned to Olympian 33 which was taken into the bodyshop for a complete overhaul, at which time various modifications to the interior were also made which included changing the seating layout to H47/25F and installing full DiPTAC features on the lower deck. The seating capacity was reduced to accommodate more luggage space with three separate pens now being provided. The mouldings on the outside were repositioned whilst repanelling work was undertaken and No. 33 was outshopped in November of that year almost to the standard of a new vehicle. In December Atlantean 154 was repainted with the offside fleetname and crest moved to a new position, below the driver's cab window. This was done to overcome the damage that was being caused to the paintwork when side adverts were changed. At the time of writing this process was still ongoing with the alteration only being effected on application of a full repaint. During 1994 similar work to that undertaken on No. 33 was carried out on Atlanteans 1 and 2. Although the latters' seating capacity has not been altered the high-backed seats have been replaced with standard bus seats with the work being completed in September and May respectively. As a private organisation the company has not been hesitant in looking outside for additional bus repair and maintenance work and this led in July to a commitment to paint a number of ex-Yorkshire Rider vehicles on behalf of G.M. Buses North. The numbers involved

eventually amounted to four Fleetlines and three Metroriders.

In September attention was turned to the renewal of the minibus fleet with the placing of an order for ten B25F Optare Metroriders to be delivered in two batches; one of four for replacement of the acquired Dodges for use on the Riversway Park & Ride service, which had just been retained on open tender, with a further six to follow early in the new year for commencement of normal minibus replacement. The Park & Ride examples received dedicated P & R lettering and entered the fleet at the beginning of December as numbers 1 to 4 (M401-4TCK), whilst the balance of the order, Nos. 5-10 (M405-10TCK), followed in March '95. All ten were received in all-over ivory with the blue being applied in the Deepdale paintshop, although due to capacity problems Nos. 8 to 10 were actually pressed into service in their as-received condition but with the addition of '*Preston Mini*' fleetnames. The Metroriders replaced eleven of the first generation Dodge minibuses with Nos. 6, 8, 9 and 65 passing to Road Car at Lincoln; Nos. 7, 68/9 seeing further use with Appleby's in Bridlington and Nos. 53/5-7 moving the short distance up the M6 to Warrington B.T. The Road Car acquisitions were all painted white before despatch and similarly those purchased by Warrington were painted into its colourful yellow and blue minibus livery before collection. A further twelve Optare Metroriders with B29F bodywork were ordered early in the year for further Dodge

The acquired Dodge minibuses were replaced on the Riversway Park & Ride service in December 1994 by four 25-seat Optare Metroriders with P. & R. branding. First of the batch, No. 1, is seen the following month about to leave the car park for the Fishergate area of town. In consequence of the fleet numbers of Atlanteans 1 and 2 were renumbered to 181/2.

Six more Metroriders entered service in March 1995 numbered 5-10. No. 5 is seen as delivered on 3rd March, parked alongside the minibus compound, and although this particular bus received blue relief before entering service the last three were temporarily pressed into service with only the addition of fleetnames and legal lettering.

replacements during the 1995/96 financial year. The first eight, Nos. 20-7 (N420-7GBV), entered service at the beginning of October with five of the type being dedicated to service 19. As recorded previously several Olympians and the Lynxes were renumbered as part of a general renumbering scheme which also included Atlanteans Nos. 1 and 2, which became 181/2 in 11/94, and the Tiger coach which was first re-registered PRN909 in 12/94 and then renumbered 309 in 3/95. As a result of the latter the PD3 training bus was reregistered PFF997 before its disposal for preservation. Following government legislation which came into effect from 1st April 1995, all buses used on school work henceforth had to display a specified sign on the front and back of the vehicle. Unlike some fleets whose buses received blanket coverage of the signs, Preston selected just 17

Atlanteans comprising Nos. 143/7/8, 151-9, 161/2/4/6 and 173, which were deemed sufficient to cover current school contract requirements; they also continued to be used on ordinary stage work at which time the signs could be folded over. Five of these were delicensed at the beginning of August as being surplus to requirements during the school summer holidays. In July the last double-deck full-height rear adverts were all removed with Olympians Nos. 101/32 receiving back end repaints and 103 being specially treated to a full repaint, the result of which can be seen on the front cover of this book.

On a final note, with only another nine years to go before the Company celebrates its centenary, it is to be hoped that the smartly turned out blue and ivory buses will be around for many more years to come to continue to brighten up the streets of Preston.

Preston Bus, like all operators, has to watch expenditure very closely. Engineering is one area where savings can be made at overhaul by innovation and the replacement of expensive components with in-house manufactured alternatives. A good example can be seen with Leyland Lynx No. 229 which has been considerably modified under the watchful eye of bodyshop foreman Derek Fullerton. Sheet aluminium has replaced expensive plastic-moulded components on the front, giving savings of several hundred pounds in this area alone. A simpler form of external wheel arch has also been incorporated.

Bus and Tram Fleet List

TRAMS

Nos	Trucks	Builder	Motors	Seating	New	Wdn	Notes
1-26	Brill 21E 6' 0"	Dick Kerr	DK25A	O26/22	1904	1929-35	
27-30	Brill 22E Bogies	Dick Kerr	DK34A	O38/30	1904	1929-34	
31-3	Brill 39E Bogies	U. E. Car Co.	DK9A3	40	1912	1935	
34-9	Preston Fexible	U. E. Car Co.	DK9A3	30/22	1914	1935	
40-5	Brill 21E	U. E. Car Co.	DK25A	28	1919	1927-35	New 1901-3, ex Sheffield CT
46-8	Brill 21E	Brush	DK25A	28	1920	1935	New 1900, ex Sheffield CT; 48 renumbered 12 in 1929
30, 40/2	P'tn Standard	P'ton Corporation	DK94/1C	30/22	1925-7	1934	Built from parts from various cars
13/8, 22	Brill 21E	English Electric	DK30B	30/22	1929	1935	New 1919, ex Lincoln CT

BUSES

Fleet Nos	Reg Nos	Chassis	Body	Seating	New	Wdn	Notes
Pre-War							
51-3	CK3446/5/7	Leyland G7	English Electric	B30D	1922	1931	
54	CK3512	Leyland G7	English Electric	B30D	1923	1931	
55-9	CK3563/4/0-2	Leyland SG7	English Electric	B36D	1924	1933	55/6/9 to B32D c1/29
60/1	CK3629/30	Leyland A13	English Electric	B22D	1925	1933	
62	CK3631	Leyland SG9	English Electric	B26D	1925	1936	
63/4	CK3746/5	Leyland PLSP1	English Electric	H52R	1926	1934	
65	CK3907	Leyland PLSP2	English Electric	H54R	1927	1934	
66	CK4050	Leyland TD1	Leyland	L24/24RO	1928	1938	
67	CK4172	Leyland TD1	Leyland	L24/24RO	1929	1940	
71-4	CK4173-6	Leyland LT1	Leyland	B35F	1929	1939	Used as Ambulances during WW2
51/2	CK4601/2	Leyland TD1	Leyland	H29/24R	1931	1947/40	
41-50	CK4637-44/6/7	Leyland TD2	English Electric	H29/24R	1932	1947/51	41/3-7/9 rebodied by E.E. in 1940
75-8	CK4648-51	Leyland LT5	English Electric	B32R	1932	1941-52	76 to Mobile Library 9/48
53	CK4702	Leyland TD2	English Electric	H27/24R	1933	1951	Rebodied by E.E. 1939/40
68-70	CK4703-5	Leyland TD2	English Electric	H28/24R	1933	1948/51	69 rebodied by E.E. 1939/40; 70 was H26/24R
79	CK4706	Leyland LT5	English Electric	B32R	1933	1953	
80	CK4707	Leyland TS4	English Electric	B32R	1933	1954	
54-9	CK4792-7	Leyland TD3	English Electric	H29/24R	1933	1950-7	55/6/8 rebodied by Croft in 3/45
1-10	CK4921-30	Leyland TD3c	English Electric	L26/26R	1934	1939/47-57	1, 9 rebodied by Croft in 3/45; 4 accident victim 4/39
60	OF3959	Leyland TD1	Leyland	L27/24R	1935	1937	New 1/29, ex Ley D/strator
61	TJ3278	Leyland TD3c	Leyland	H30/26R	1935	1950	New 10/33, ex Ley D/strator
11-4	RN7701-4	Leyland TD4c	Leyland	H30/24R	1935	1954/5	11 to H30/26R in 10/51
15-32	RN7705-22	Leyland TD4c	English Electric	H28/26R	1935	1947/50-7	
81/2	RN7723/4	Leyland LT7c	Leyland	B38R	1935	1954	
62-4	RN8018-20	Leyland TD4c	English Electric	H30/24R	1936	1953-7	62/4 to H30/26R in 7/52, 9/51
33-7	RN8348-52	Leyland TD5c	English Electric	H30/24R	1937/8	1950-7	33/6 used as Grandstands 1952 Guild, 34/5/7 to H30/26R 1952-4
83	RN8353	Leyland LT7c	English Electric	B38R	1937	1953	
38-40	RN8885/6/4	Leyland TD5c	Leyland	H29/26R	1939	1958	
4	RN8887	Leyland TD5c	Leyland	L27/26R	1939	1957	
65	ACK224	Leyland TD7	Leyland	H30/26R	1940	1958	
Post War							
84-9, 52	ARN388-94	Leyland PD1	Alexander	H30/26R	1946	1960-3	85/6 to Polling Booths 8/64
60/6/7	BCK25-7	Leyland PD1	Leyland	L27/26R	1946	1958/60	60/6 renumbered 8, 12 in 8/58
71-3, 90-4	BCK621-8	Leyland PD1A	Leyland	H30/26R	1947	1961-8	72/3 to Polling Booths 8/64; 91 to H32/27R in 1959
95-100	BCK629-34	Leyland PD1A	Samlesbury	H30/26R	1947	1961-8	98 to Polling Booth 8/64
101/2	BCK635/6	Leyland PD1A	Leyland	H30/26R	1947	1961/5	
103-7	BCK936-40	Leyland PD1A	Leyland	L27/26R	1947	1958/60	106/7 renumbered 6(4/57) & 7('58); 6 accident victim 5/60 & to B/D veh
74/5	CRN79, 80	Leyland PS1	East Lancs	B35R	1949	1968	74 to Polling Booth 6/70
108-27	DRN291-310	Leyland PD2/1	Leyland	H30/26R	1950/1	1967-72	110 accident victim 3/67
41-8	ECK501-8	Leyland PD2/10	Leyland	H30/28R	1952	1971	To H32/29R in 1959
2, 5	ECK509/10	Leyland PD2/10	Leyland	L28/27R	1952	1959/60	
9, 10	FRN731/2	Leyland PD2/10	Leyland	L27/28R	1954	1959/61	
49-51/3/4/7/9,61	FRN733-40	Leyland PD2/10	Leyland	H30/28R	1954	1962-76	To H32/29R in 1958/9
79-83	HRN485-9	Leyland PD2/10	Met-Cam	H32/26R	1955	1976	To H33/29R in 1962
24-8	JCK583-7	Leyland PD2/10	Crossley	H30/28R	1956	1969-75	To H33/29R in 1960/1
20-2	KCK328-30	Leyland PD2/10	Crossley	H32/26R	1957	1975	To H32/29R in 1961
23/9-37	KRN419-28	Leyland PD2/10	Crossley	H30/28R	1957	1970-6	To H32 or H33/29R in 1959-61

Fleet Nos	Reg Nos	Chassis	Body	Seating	New	Wdn	Notes
62-8	MCK293-9	Leyland PD3/5	Met-Cam	H40/32F	1958	1976-9	*67 to PD3/4 in 1972*
9	NCK741	Leyland PD3/6	Leyland/PCTD	H41/32F	1959	1977	*Rebuilt from PD2 FRN731*
5	NCK757	Leyland PD3/6	Leyland/PCTD	H38/32F	1960	1978	*Rebuilt from PD2 ECK510*
2	PRN761	Leyland PD3/6	Leyland/PCTD	H38/32F	1961	1979	*Rebuilt from PD2 ECK509*
13-9	PRN905-11	Leyland PD3/4	Met-Cam	H39/31F	1961	1977/80	*16 to B/D vehicle by 3/78*
10	PRN762	Leyland PD3/6	Leyland/PCTD	H38/32F	1962	1977	*Rebuilt from PD2 FRN732*
50/1	SRN375/6	Leyland PD3/6	Leyland/PCTD	H38/32F	1962/3	1978/7	*Rebuilt from PD2s FRN734/5*
84-90	TRN386-92	Leyland PD3A/1	Met-Cam	H39/31F	1963	1978-80	
61	BCK367C	Leyland PD3/6	Leyland/PCTD	H38/32F	1965	1978	*Rebuilt from PD2 FRN740*
69-73	ARN654-8C	Leyland PD3A/1	Met-Cam	H39/31F	1965	1980/1	
59	FCK453F	Leyland PD3/6	Leyland/PCTD	H38/32F	1967	1978	*Rebuilt from PD2 FRN739*
201-5	HCK201-5G	Leyland PSUR1A/1	Met-Cam	B47D	1968	1980/1	
206-15	HCK206-15G	Leyland PSUR1A/1	Marshall	B47D	1968	1980/1	
216-22	KRN216-22H	Leyland PSUR1A/1R	Marshall	B49D	1970	1981/2	
223-9	MCK223-9J	Leyland PSUR1B/1R	Seddon	B48D	1971	1982/3	
230-4	AUE309-13J	Leyland PSUR1A/1R	Marshall C'mair	B41D	1971	1983	*Ex Midland Red 11/71; renumbered 237-41 in 7/72; to B47D in 1980*
230-6	RTF430-6L	Leyland PSUR1B/1R	Seddon	B48D	1972	1983/4	*233/5/6 renumbered 33/5/6 in 10/83*
101-10	GBV101-10N	Leyland AN68/2R	Alexander	H49/33D	1974/5	1987/9	
242	PHG242P	Bristol LHS6L	Duple	DP31F	1976	1987	*Renumbered 342(4/77), 42(10/83)*
243/4	PHG243/4P	Bristol LHS6L	Duple	B31F	1976	1987	*Renumbered 343/4(4/77), 43/4(10/83)*
111-20	UFV111-20R	Leyland AN68/2R	East Lancs	H50/32D	1976	1989/90	
121-30	CRN121-30S	Leyland AN68A/2R	East Lancs	H50/32D	1977/8	1990/1	
131-40	NCK131-40T	Leyland AN68A/2R	East Lancs	H50/32D	1978/9	1992	
141-50	UHG141-50V	Leyland AN68A/2R	Alexander	H49/33D	1980		*Rebuilt to H49/36F 1991-3*
151-7	GFV151-7W	Leyland AN68B/2R	East Lancs	H50/32D	1981		*Rebuilt to H50/36F 1990-3*
158-65	OBV158-65X	Leyland AN68C/2R	East Lancs	H50/32D	1981		*Rebuilt to H50/36F 1990-2*
166-72	URN166-72Y	Leyland AN68D/2R	East Lancs	H50/32D	1982		*Rebuilt to H50/36F 1990/1*
173-7	DRN173-7Y	Leyland AN68D/2R	East Lancs	H50/32D	1983		*Rebuilt to H50/36F 1990/1*
1, 2	DRN1, 2Y	Leyland AN68D/2R	East Lancs	CH45/29F	1983		*To H45/29F in 5/94(2) & 9/94(1); renumbered 181/2 in 11/94*
3	A33MRN	Leyland ON	ECW	CH47/27F	1984		*Used as D/strator 5/84-7/85, renum 33 in 2/85, 133 in 3/95; to H47/25F in 10/93*
5-8	YFY1,2.7.8M	Leyland Nat 1151/2R	Leyland	B49F	1986	1987/9	*New to Southport CT 1974, ex MPTE in 8/86; 6 accident victim 7/87*
50-66	D750-66YCW	Dodge S56	N.Counties	B22F	1987	1995-	
67	D767YCW	Dodge S56	N.Counties	DP20F	1987		*Reseated to B20F in 1/94*
68/9	D768/9YCW	Dodge S46	N.Counties	B22F	1987	1994	
70/1	D870/1ABV	Dodge S56	N.Counties	DP20F	1987		
40	D40AFV	Leyland Tiger CTL11	Duple	C51F	1987		*Re-registered PRN909 in 12/94, renum 309 in 3/95*
41-3	D41-3AFV	Dodge S56	N.Counties	B22F	1987	1995/-	
72-4	D72-4AFV	Dodge S56	N.Counties	B22F	1987	1995/-	
44	E44FFV	Dodge S56	N.Counties	B20F	1987		*Reseated to B22F in 10/87*
45/6	E45/6GRN	Dodge S56	N.Counties	B22F	1987	1995/-	
47	E47KBV	Renault S56	N.Counties	B25F	1988		
75-7	E75-7LFR	Renault S56	N.Counties	B25F	1988		
48/9	E48/9MCK	Renault S56	N.Counties	B25F	1988		
78-87	E78-87MHG	Renault S56	N.Counties	B25F	1988		
88-90	F88-90UHG	Renault S56	N.Counties	B25F	1988		
10/1	F210/1YHG	Leyland Lynx Mk 1	Leyland	B47F	1989		*Renumbered 210/1 in 2/95*
12/3	F212/3YHG	Leyland Lynx Mk 1	Leyland	DP45F	1989		*Renumbered 212(3/95) & 213(2/95)*
32	F32AHG	Leyland ON	N.Counties	H51/34F	1989		*Renumbered 132 in 2/95*
91/2	F91/2AHG	Renault S56	N.Counties	B25F	1989		
14-8	G214-8KRN	Leyland Lynx Mk 1	Leyland	DP45F	1989		*Renumbered 214-8 in 2/95*
34/5	G34/5OCK	Leyland ON	Leyland	CH43/29F	1990		*Renumbered 134(3/95) & 135(4/95)*
36/7	G36/7OCK	Leyland ON	Leyland	H47/31F	1990		*Renumbered 136/7 in 4/95*
23/4/6-9	H23/4/6-9YBV	Leyland Lynx Mk 1	Leyland	DP45F	1990		*Renumbered 223(2/95), 224(3/95) & 226-9(2/95)*
6	D456BEO	Dodge S56	East Lancs	B22F	1991	1995	*New to Barrow CT 12/86, ex Magicbus in 1/91*
7	D32SAO	Dodge S56	Reeve Burgess	B23F	1991	1994	*New 10/86, ex Cumberland MS 1/91*
8, 9	D458/9BEO	Dodge S56	East Lancs	DP22F	1991	1995/4	*New to Barrow CT 12/86, ex Stagecoach / Magicbus in 1/91*
101-4	H101-4BFR	Leyland ON	N.Counties	H47/30F	1991		
106	J976PRW	Leyland ON	Leyland	H47/31F	1991		*Used by Ley Volvo as D/strator*
107	J107KCW	Leyland ON	Leyland	CH43/29F	1991		*Guild '92 Promotional Vehicle*
108-10/2/3	J108-10/2/3KCW	Leyland ON	Leyland	H47/31F	1992		
114	J114KCW	Leyland ON	Leyland	CH43/29F	1992		
1-4	M401-4TCK	Optare MR	Optare	B25F	1994		*Park & Ride lettering*
5-10	M405-10TCK	Optare MR	Optare	B25F	1995		
20-31	N420-31GBV	Optare MR	Optare	B29F	1995/6		

APPENDIX B

Standard Livery Applications

Type		Description	Period	Vehicles as delivered
Pre-war				
Trams	(1)	Various arrangements of maroon & cream with lining out	1904-1935	
Single-deck buses	(2)	Cream with maroon waistband & engine cover / full lining out	1922-1929	G7s, SGs, A13s
	(3)	Maroon with cream waistband, window surrounds & roof / full lining out	1929-1940	LTs & TS
Double-deck buses	(4)	Maroon with 3 cream bands, cream window surrounds & roof / full lining out	1926-1933	PLSPs, TD1/2s
	(5)	Maroon with 3 cream bands & roof between domes / full lining out	1933-1940	TD3-5/7s
Post war				
Single-deck buses	(6)	Maroon roof (except domes) and below waistrail, remainder cream	1946-1966	PS1s (see note ii)
	(7)	Blue with ivory as (6)	1966-1968	PS1s (repainted)
	(8)	Ivory with blue roof, skirt & doors	1968 to date	Panthers, Ley Nats$, Lynxes
Double-deck buses	(9)	Maroon with cream bands below upper/lower deck windows & between decks	1946-1949	PD1/As
	(10)	Maroon with cream window surrounds to both decks	1950-1951	PD2/1s
	(11)	Maroon with cream lower deck window surrounds	1952-1955	Leyland & MCW bodied PD2/10s
	(12)	All maroon with a single cream band above the lower deck windows	1956-1966	Crossley bodied PD2/10s, PD3s*
	(13)	Blue with ivory window surrounds & between decks band	1966-1973	PD3/6 No 59 (see note v)
	(14)	Ivory with blue skirt, doors roof & between decks band	1973 to date	AN68s, Olympians
Minibuses	(15)	Ivory with blue roof, window surrounds & skirt	1976-1987	LHSs
	(16)	Ivory with blue roof & skirt	1987 to date	Dodges, Metroriders

Notes		
	(i)	In the period 1946 to c1957 several TDs and PD1s sported more than one of the post war maroon & cream livery applications.
	(ii)	Those LTs & the TS which survived into the post war era also received livery application (6)
	(iii)	All the PD1s, PD2s & PD3s (except PD3 No 59) eventually wore livery application (12).
	(iv)	PD3/6 No 59 was the only bus received new in livery application (13).
	(v)	Livery application (13) was later applied to PD2s Nos 20-4/9, 31-7, 41-9, 53/4/7, 79-83, 122-6 & the rest of the PD3s.
	(vi)	All the PD3s eventually received livery application (14).
	(vii)	$ The Leyland Nationals originally entered service in MPTE jonquil green & cream with a brown skirt.
	(viii)	Metroriders 8-10 initially entered service with no blue relief.
	(ix)	The G7s carried PRESTON CORPORATION fleetnames; a fleetname was not reintroduced until 1974.
	(x)	The town crest was applied to the buses on its own from 1924 to 1974.

APPENDIX C

Service Renumberings (with no alteration to route)

P to BR	c Dec. 1935	FP to 16	3 Nov. 1980	P1/P3 to 29	3 Nov. 1980
FR to P1	1 Jan. 1948	FR to 36	3 Nov. 1980	P2 to 28	3 Nov. 1980
GL to FR	1 Jan. 1948	G to 12	3 Nov. 1980	P4 to 34	3 Nov. 1980
M to MN	8 Mar. 1952	GL to 10	3 Nov. 1980	P6 to 43	3 Nov. 1980
A to 24	3 Nov. 1980	HS to 14	3 Nov. 1980	P7 to 30	3 Nov. 1980
BF to 36	3 Nov. 1980	LS to 36	3 Nov. 1980	7 to 8	21 Oct. 1985
BR to 21	3 Nov. 1980	MN to 7	3 Nov. 1980	35 to 5	25 Nov. 1985
CR to 35	3 Nov. 1980	PL to 22	3 Nov. 1980	36 to 6	25 Nov. 1985
D to 15	3 Nov. 1980	P1 to 27	3 Nov. 1980	37 to 7	25 Nov. 1985
F to 20	3 Nov. 1980	P3 to 26	3 Nov. 1980	28 to 32	13 July 1987

APPENDIX D

Dates of Introduction and Withdrawal of Stage Services

Route	Destination	Date Service Inaugurated	Converted to PAYB	Last Day of Operation	Length (miles)	Notes
A /24	Pedders Lane Ashton	9 July. 1904	6 May 1971 #	24 Jun. 1984		(i)
A	Ashton (Lane Ends)	5 Jun. 1924		10 Nov. 1946		
B	Ashton Inkerman Street	11 Nov. 1946		11 Feb. 1965		
B	Ashton (Lane Ends)	7 Aug. 1934		10 Nov. 1946		
BF/36/ 6	Brookfield via Deepdale	24 July 1958	2 Dec. 1968		3.35	(ii)
BR/21	Broadgate	30 Jun. 1904	2 Dec. 1968		1.50	
C	Cemetery and Lane Ends	19 Sept. 1932		11 Dec. 1939		
C	Lane Ends Ashton	-- Nov. 1937	1 Dec. 1972 #	2 Nov. 1980		(i)
CL	Callon Estate	30 Aug. 1976		1 July 1977		
CR/35/ 5	Brookfield via Cromwell Road	8 Mar. 1952	2 Dec. 1968	14 Oct. 1989		(iii)
D	Ashton Lane Ends	11 Nov. 1946		31 Dec. 1947		
D /15	Fulwood via Deepdale	30 Jun. 1904	2 Dec. 1968	12 Jun. 1983		
F /20	Fulwood via North Road	7 Jun. 1904	2 Dec. 1968	12 Jun. 1983		
FP/16	Farringdon Park	7 Jun. 1904	22 Mar. 1982		2.20	
FR/P1,P3/29	Frenchwood	5 Jun. 1924	6 Apr. 1970	15 Oct. 1989		
G /12	Grange Estate via Moor Nook	30 Aug. 1976		24 Oct. 1986		
GL/FR/36	Gamull Lane or Fulwood Row	15 Apr. 1937	2 Dec. 1968	12 Jun. 1983		
GL/10	Ribbleton Gamull Lane	1 Jan. 1948	30 Aug. 1976	12 July 1987		
HS/14	Holme Slack	17 Feb. 1936	14 Jan. 1980		2.10	
LEC	Cemetery and Lane Ends	10 Apr. 1925		by Jan. 1958		(iv)
LS/36/ 6	Longsands Lane	15 Apr. 1937	2 Dec. 1968	12 July 1987		
M /MN/ 7/ 8	Moorside or Moor Nook	10 July 1939	3 Dec. 1971 #		3.00	(i)
M	Moor Nook	8 Mar. 1952		by Jan. 1958		
P	Penwortham	See BR Broadgate				
PL/22	Lytham Road or Boys Lane or Queens Drive or Fulwood	23 Jan. 1922	7 Aug. 1978		3.60	
R	Ribbleton Chatburn Road	26 Jan. 1905		31 Dec. 1947		
TS	Trafford Street	12 May 1947		31 Dec. 1947		
P1/P3/26	Lea (via Waterloo Road)	1 Jan. 1948	6 Apr. 1970	2 Nov. 1980 *		(v)
P1/27	Larches Estate	4 Apr. 1955	6 Apr. 1970		3.90	
P2/28	Lightfoot Lane	1 Jan. 1948	4 Apr. 1970 $	12 Jun. 1983		(vi)
P3	Lea via Waterloo Road	See P1/P3/26				
P4	Penwortham Crookings Lane	1 Jan. 1948		30 Apr. 1948		
P4/34	Ingol (via Fylde Road)	13 Feb. 1965	1 Oct. 1976		3.70	
P5	Hutton Anchor Inn	1 Jan. 1948		11 May 1979		
P6/43	Ingol Redcar Avenue	12 Nov. 1973	3 Nov. 1980	8 Apr. 1988		
P7/30	Savick Estate Luton Road	14 Oct. 1974	30 Aug. 1976	18 Apr. 1987		
3	Longton	15 May 1989		16 Sept. 1989		
4	Penwortham	16 May 1988		15 Oct. 1989		
5	Longsands Lane	16 Oct. 1989			3.55	
9	Moor Nook (via Miller Road)	16 Oct. 1989			3.40	
10	Gamull Lane / Roman Way	16 Oct. 1989		19 Jan. 1990		
10	Gamull Lane via Grange	10 Dec. 1992			3.50	
11	Ribbleton Gamull Lane	13 Jun. 1983			2.65	
13	Inner Link	9 Oct. 1982		8 Jan. 1983		
15	Sherwood via Deepdale	13 Jun. 1983		12 July 1987		
17, 126	Bamber Bridge or Clayton Gn. ASDA	16 May 1988		15 Oct. 1989		
19	Royal Preston Hospital	21 Apr. 1987			3.80	
20	Sherwood via Garstang Road	13 Jun. 1983		12 July 1987		
23, 123	Sherwood / ASDA	13 July 1987			4.40/5.25	
24	Conway Drive	17 Aug. 1987		9 Oct. 1987		
24	Lea Hawthorn Crescent	5 Dec. 1988			4.20	
25	Lea via Tulketh Road	25 Jun. 1984			3.80	
26	Lea via Garstang Road	3 Nov. 1980		24 Jun. 1984		
28/32	Tanterton via Garstang Road	13 Jun. 1983			5.35	
29	Savick Estate	28 Jan. 1991			4.25	
30	Savick Estate (via Fylde Road)	21 Apr. 1987			4.40	
31	Savick Estate (via Brook Street)	16 Oct. 1989			4.35	
31	Broughton / Woodplumpton	9 Nov. 1987		13 Oct. 1989		
33	Tanterton via Brook Street	3 Nov. 1980			3.95	
35	Tanterton via Fylde Road	16 Oct. 1989			3.85	
37/ 7	Fulwood Row via Garstang Road	13 Jun. 1983			3.70	
39	Preston and Blackpool	16 July 1988		18 Nov. 1988		
43	Ingol via Mill Lane	11 Apr. 1988			4.00	
44	Ingol via Brook Street	3 Nov. 1980			3.85	
114	Holme Slack (Fairfax Road)	11 May 1987			2.70	
127	Larches Estate / Lea	1 Feb. 1988			4.30	

Notes :-
(i)	# Initially on M-SO, Su from 5 Sept. '76
(ii)	Service withdrawn 13/7/87 to 11/10/87
(iii)	Service suspended 9/9/70 to 3/9/73; withdrawn 13/7/87 to 10/4/88
(iv)	Service suspended 12/39 to –/46
(V)	*Except two am. journeys inwards on M - F
(vi)	$ Back to crew 17 Apr. '78 & to PAYB(2nd) 7 Aug. '78
(vii)	Route lengths are for 1994

APPENDIX E

Special Liveries and Advert Buses

Reg.	Veh.	Livery Details	Dates
Special Liveries			
CK4707	80	National Child Safety Week	1954 (as wdn)
KRN424	33	Exp. Blue / Ivory livery	1966/67
ECK503	43	Exp. Oxford Blue / White livery	1966/67
HRN487	81	Exp. Light Blue / White livery	1966/67
RTF436L	(2)36	Red Rose Rambler Ticket	10/82 to 8/84
DRN1,2Y	1,2	Blue and Ivory with Blue Stripes	6/83 to 6/90(1)
			7/90(2)
A33MRN	(3)3	As DRN 1,2Y / Ley D/strator lettering	2/84 to 6/90
D40AFV	40	As DRN 1,2Y(Coach Version)	
D456BEO	6	All White	2/91 to 11/92
		Riversway Park & Ride	11/92 to 1/95
J107KCW	107	Guild '92	10/91 to 1/93
Allover Advert Buses			
TRN390	88	Dorman Smith / Guild 72	4/72 to 9/72
HRN485	79	Metro '76	5/76(as wdn)
UFV115R	115	Matthew Brown Brewery	9/79 to 6/81
CRN128S	128	Hitchens Kitchens	10/84 to 11/85
GFV153W	153#	Slalom Lager	4/81 to 6/82
OBV160X	160	Harlequin Chocolates	3/84 to 8/85
OBV165X	165	Whitegates Estate Agents	7/86 to 5/88
URN166Y	166	Martin Dawes	10/86 to 12/87
URN171Y	171	Bellway Homes	10/85 to 12/86
URN172Y	172#	Matthew Brown Lion Bitter	11/82 to 6/85
DRN177Y	177	Matthew Brown slalom D	4/85 to 5/87
		Homebuyers Advice Centre	11/90 to 12/91
		British Nuclear Fuels Ltd.*	1/92 to 10/93
D458BEO	8	Fishergate Shopping Centre	2/91 to 4/94
D459BEO	9	St. Georges Shopping Centre	2/91 to 4/92
D42AFV	42	Wintershield Glass*	6/91 to 7/95
E49MCK	49	Ladbroke Computing International*	11/93
E80MHG	80	British Nuclear Fuels Ltd.*	12/91 to 7/93
E82MHG	82	Vine House Cancer Appeal*	10/94
E83MHG	83	Ladbroke Computing International*	11/90
E85MHG	85	Derian House Hospice Appeal*	2/92
G35OCK	35	Guild 92*	4/91 to 2/93
G36OCK	(1)36	Smoke Free Campaign (P.H.A.)*	8/92
G37OCK	(1)37	Wintershield Glass*	8/91 to 5/95
	137	A Healthy Preston (P.H.A.)*	6/95
H104BFR	104	Sharoe Green Maternity Unit (P.H.A.)*	6/93

(i) *Adverts were not applied to the front of the vehicle, which retained fleet livery.

(ii) # ANs 153/72 were delivered in white & red base colours respectively.

Full Height Rear Adverts

Reg.	Veh.	Livery Details	Dates
URN166Y	166	Lookers Grosvenor	2/88 to c6/92
A33MRN	33	Transad Bus Advertising	6/91 to 11/93
E76LFR	76	Clutch Clinic	8/92
F32AHG	(1)32	Gillies Tool & Plant Hire	8/91 to 7/95
H101BFR	101	Clutch Clinic	8/92 to 7/95
H102BFR	102	Clutch Clinic	8/92 to 6/95
H103BFR	103	Howick House Local Blind Society	12/92 to 7/95

APPENDIX F

Vehicles Operated on Loan

Date	Reg.	Make	Owner
1959	398JTB	Ley PDR1 / MCW	Ley Motors D/strator
Aug-66	CRH173C	Ley PSUR / Roe	K-u-Hull CT
1967	YTB771D	Ley PSURC / Strns	Ley Motors D/strator
Feb-71	VWD451H	Scania / MCW	Scania D/strator
Apr-72	XKC831K	Ley AN68 / Alex	Merseyside PTE
Jul-72	DAO851K	Ley National	Ley Motors D/strator
Aug-72	FRM499K	Ley National	Ley Motors D/strator
Sep-72	OTF360K*	Bristol Re / ECW	Ribble Motors
Sep-72	CTB166-8E*	Ley PD3A / EL	Accrington CT
Sep-72	STB790/2G*	Ley PDR1A / EL	Accrington CT
Sep-72	HTF176-8K*	Ley PDR1A / EL	Accrington CT
Sep-72	RTB797L*	Ley PDR1A / EL	Accrington CT
Sep-72	KBV49-52F*	Ley PDR1A / EL	Blackburn CT
Sep-72	KBV54F*	Ley PDR1A / EL	Blackburn CT
Sep-72	PCB77-9J*	Ley PDR1A / EL	Blackburn CT
Sep-72	TTE641/2D*	Ley PDR1 / MCW	J Fishwick & Sons
Sep-72	PCK382*	Ley PD3 / MCW	Ribble Motors
Sep-72	RCK907*	Ley PD3 / MCW	Ribble Motors
Sep-72	398JTB*	Ley PDR1 / MCW	Ribble Motors
1974	VEB566L	Volvo / Mar Cam	Volvo D/strator
Jul-77	XCW955R	Ley National	Ley Motors D/strator
May-79	FBF129T	Den Dom / EL	East Staff DC
Jun-79	BCK706R	Ley Titan	Ley Veh D/strator
Feb-81	NHG732P	Ley Titan	Ley Veh D/strator
May-81	DFR979W	Ley Lep / Duple	Ley Veh D/strator
Jun-81	VCW85V	Ley Lep / Pn	Ley Veh D/strator
May-84	EBV86S	Ley AN68 / NCME	Fylde BT
Mar-87	D861/2LWR	Fr Rov / Dorm	Yorkshire Rider
Mar-87	D912NBA	Dodge S56 / NCME	NCME / D/strator
May-87	B417CMC	Ley Tiger / Pn	Blackburn BT
May-87	UBV85L	Ley AN68 / EL	Lancaster CT
Dec-87	E38OMS	Dodge S56 / Alex	Alexander / D/strator
Oct-88	E26ECH	Scania / Alex	Scania / D/strator
Dec-88	HPY318N	Ford / NCME	Lancaster CT
Dec-88	BTO291T	Bed Vas / Pn	Lancaster CT
Jun-91	H401DMJ	Ren S75 / Rv Bur	Renault / D/strator
Jun-91	H398SYG	Optare (MCW)MR	Optare / D/strator
Jul-92	J215OCW	Den Lan / NCME	NCME / D/strator
Aug-92	J120SPF	Den Lan / Plaxton	Plaxton / D/strator
Aug-92	UBV84L*	Ley AN68 / EL	Lancaster CT
Aug-92	J110SPB	Den Lan / Alex	Dennis / D/strator
Sep-92	J363BNW	Optare (MCW)MR	Optare / D/strator
Sep-92	GBV109/10N*	Ley AN68 / Alex	Hyndburn BT
Sep-92	NRN383P*	Ley AN68 / PR	Hyndburn BT
Sep-92	DDK25W*	Ley AN68 / EL	Rossendale BT
Sep-92	HIL3188*	Ley ON / EL	Rossendale BT
Sep-93	K112SRH	Den Dart / Pn	London Buses
Mar-94	L478TDU	Volvo B6 / Alex	Volvo / D/strator
Apr-94	L836MWT	Optare (MCW)MR	Optare / D/strator
Aug-94	L708LKY	Merc Benz / Wright	Mercedes / D/strator
Dec-94	L416PAR	Den Dart/Marshall	Marshall / D/strator

(i) This list is not thought to be conclusive although most vehicle loans have taken place in the last 25 years or so.

(ii) * Vehicles marked thus were hired specifically for the '72 & '92 Guilds respectively